THE KENNEDY GOVERNMENT

By Stan Opotowsky

THE LONGS OF LOUISIANA
TV: THE BIG PICTURE
THE KENNEDY GOVERNMENT

THE
KENNEDY
GOVERNMENT

by STAN OPOTOWSKY

1961

E. P. DUTTON CO., INC.
NEW YORK

Published simultaneously in Canada by
Clarke, Irwin & Co., Ltd., of Toronto

Library of Congress Catalog Card Number: 61-12465

TO
GRACE

CONTENTS

THE KENNEDY GOVERNMENT

MAKING A GOVERNMENT

Two weeks after the 1960 Democratic National Convention John Kennedy sat in his Washington home, musing about the forthcoming campaign, when suddenly an awesome thought struck him: He might win. He might actually become President of the United States.

Then what? How do you form a government? How do you run it?

The largest organization Kennedy had ever run was the 21-man staff he employed as Senator. The next largest organization he had ever directed was the crew of a PT boat. He had never been a governor or even the manager of a supermarket. The President of the United States directs a staff of 2,350,000.

Kennedy placed a hurried telephone call to an old friend, Clark Clifford, a Washington attorney. Clark would know how the White House operates. He had worked for Harry Truman.

That conversation was the first step in the formation of the Kennedy administration. From it came this plan: Clifford would begin immediately compiling a report on the things which must be done to launch a new administration. On the day following the election, he would either deliver the report to Kennedy or toss it into the garbage can, depending upon the decision of the voters.

Kennedy then switched his attention to the more immedi-

11

ate problem of winning the election. He concentrated on that and that alone until two days after the ballots were cast.

On that morning he called a meeting of his full staff at his summer home in Hyannis Port, Massachusetts. Now the true ordeal was to begin. Now the promises had to be fulfilled and the world crises dealt with rather than discussed.

"Our whole attitude suddenly changed," said one staff member who was present. "When Jack came into the room he was no longer 'Jack.' He was the President of the United States. We all stood up—even his brother, Bobby. It was just an instinctive thing. We seemed to realize that what lay ahead was much bigger than what had gone before."

Kennedy told his staff of the Clifford report. He hadn't actually seen it yet, but he had been given an idea of what to expect. The report totaled 50 pages. It listed 5,000 jobs which must be filled—80 of them top-level policy-making positions and 400 others secondary but also policy-making jobs.

The talent search was launched on the spot. "I want the best men we can find," Kennedy said. "If they've been our friends, fine, but primarily I want the best men." He told Sargent Shriver, his brother-in-law, and Larry O'Brien, his political expert, to take command. This was to be a mammoth undertaking that soon would embrace not only the entire staff but all of Kennedy's friends and many persons he had not yet even met.

Within weeks the President-elect's talent scouts were bogged down in despair. For one thing, there came the sudden realization that Kennedy's closest acquaintances in Washington and in Boston were either Congressmen, journalists, or prosperous businessmen. These were the three poorest groups from which to form a government. The Congressmen did not want to take administrative jobs which would cut them off from their local electorates; they considered these jobs political dead ends. The journalists considered themselves observers and critics of the government; they had no desire to become participants. The businessmen were unwilling to take the income cuts which were inevitable with government service; many were especially frightened away by the prospects of selling long-cherished securities in order to avoid any conflict-of-interest accusations.

It is partly because of this that the Kennedy Administration wound up so heavily populated with college professors. Kennedy's preference for intellectuals in government is no sham. However, their presence in such numbers on his staff is more a case of their being the best men he could get. The college professors as a rule didn't have to worry about pay cuts when they joined the government. For many it meant a pay raise. As a result, the first Kennedy appointments so depleted the faculty of the new President's alma mater that James Reston of the *New York Times* wrote, "There's nothing left at Harvard except Radcliffe," and Harvard Law School Dean Erwin Griswold sought to arrange a "no raiding pact" with the new administration. When Archibald Cox was hired from the faculty to become Solicitor General, Harvard decided to offer his job to Attorney Willard Wirtz. But when Wirtz was asked to go to Cambridge to discuss the matter he wired back that he didn't have time. He had just been appointed Undersecretary of Labor.

Despite the difficulties, Kennedy continued to insist that his staff find top-flight men. Originally he had planned to select his entire cabinet within a month after the election and to announce their appointments all on the same day. Now that was out of the question. He knew he was in for a long, hard pull.

He kept asking for suggestions from everyone he met. At

the same time he was barraged with unsolicited nominations from Democratic Party officials of all ranks. Every name was checked. O'Brien and Bob Kennedy holed up in Washington while the President-elect vacationed in Palm Beach. They investigated the background of every man suggested, working 14, 16, 18 hours a day, telephoning from one end of the nation to the other and even once to Pakistan. "There's a terrible sense of not having enough time," complained one of the men employed in the talent search. "We just don't know enough people."

Despite the close campaign and the consequent need to corral every vote and please every county chairman, Kennedy had emerged amazingly unfettered: He had not made a single firm promise of a job to anyone for anyone in the entire pre-election period.

This gave him a free hand for the ultimate appointments, but there were still pay-off problems. Adlai Stevenson, who had campaigned faithfully, wanted to be Secretary of State and, furthermore, he had strong support from an important wing of the party. Governor G. Mennen Williams of Michigan, the man who swung his state's large convention vote to Kennedy, wanted to be Secretary of Health, Education and Welfare. Franklin D. Roosevelt, Jr., had helped Kennedy win the vital West Virginia primary, and now New York Democrats were urging an especially important position for young FDR, in hopes that he might be built up as a strong candidate for governor.

Kennedy had said before he won the Democratic nomination that he thought any Democratic President "should consider Adlai Stevenson as one of his leading candidates for Secretary of State." Well, Stevenson might be a "leading candidate" now, but he certainly wasn't going to become Secretary of State. Kennedy didn't want him. The Kennedy people thought Stevenson had welched on several promises to endorse Kennedy for the nomination before the convention. Kennedy was not personally fond of Stevenson and it was also clear that Stevenson had no great love for John Kennedy. The new President had his own ideas about foreign policy and did not relish the prospect of debating them with Adlai Stevenson behind closed doors before being able to present them publicly.

It was obvious then that Stevenson would not be Secretary of State. It was just as obvious that Kennedy dare not exclude Stevenson from the administration. The Kennedy forces began negotiating through an intermediary, a Washington attorney who is a close friend of Stevenson. This didn't please Stevenson. "Why doesn't he come directly to me?" he snorted once.

Someone in the Kennedy organization suggested a way out of the dilemma: Make Stevenson Attorney General. This would establish him in a major job yet keep him clear of the State Department. It would be an appointment that the party liberals could not oppose because of their devotion to Stevenson and yet it would be an appointment which the party's Southern wing would endorse since Stevenson is not exactly militant on the subject of civil rights.

The idea, however, was rejected as impractical, and Stevenson was offered the position of Ambassador to the United Nations. Stevenson is an eloquent man, and the UN has need of his eloquence. Stevenson is greatly respected by European and Asian diplomats and government officials; he has more prestige abroad than he enjoys in his own country.

The problem of "Soapy" Williams was similar. A new law prevented him from running for re-election as governor of Michigan, and he was eager for the Health, Education and Welfare portfolio. But he was not the type of man Kennedy needed. Kennedy had firm ideas about the legislation he wanted in this field, and Williams would be only a liability. The conservatives in Congress would be difficult enough to manage without tempting them with a target in the person of ultra-liberal Williams, a close friend and political ally of Walter Reuther.

Williams was induced to take a lesser job, Undersecretary of State for Africa. It was not difficult to convince him of this position's importance with the emergence of new African republics and their important status in the balance of world power. There was more trouble in placing young Roosevelt, who wanted to be Secretary of Labor but was turned down by the unions. Then he was proposed as Secretary of the Navy but was turned down by the new Defense Secretary. Next he was considered for Undersecretary of State for Latin America, but rejected again, in this instance because his law firm had represented Dominican dictator Trujillo.

As Kennedy and his staff picked and bickered and cajoled their way through the task of building an administration, the thorniest problem was also the most touching: What to do with Bobby Kennedy?

He is a brilliant young lawyer, a likable chap, a man who quickly attained prominence and success in the government, and, what's more, he was politically deserving as the successful candidate's campaign manager. Under ordinary circumstances such a man would have quickly plucked the government job he desired and not an eyebrow would have been raised. But the fact that Bobby Kennedy was the President-elect's brother, and only a 35-year-old brother at that, presented a ticklish problem.

At first Bobby Kennedy decided to take the easy way out. He would accept no government job and thus risk no criticism of himself or his brother. He even announced this flatly on a nationwide television program.

It was true he had prepared himself in college for government service and had never before wanted or considered anything else. But, he thought, he might still serve his ambitions by running for governor of Massachusetts or maybe Senator.

Later he said, "I made the decision and then I set out to help my brother bring in the people he would need for his administration. I found it a lot more difficult than I had imagined. A number of people had talked to us often about getting good and honest men in government. When we went to them we couldn't get them to serve.

"So I began thinking again about staying in the government. My brother talked to me about it several times and urged me to take a job of some sort.

"I thought of the problems that lay ahead. I realized our biggest problem would be with the Soviet Union, so I thought about going into the Defense Department or the State Department, not at the top but in a position where I might do some good."

Gradually Bobby Kennedy came around to the feeling that he could take a job in his brother's administration. It was only a matter of finding the right one, the one which would draw the least criticism. A friend who called upon him at the time asked his plans and Bobby replied, "Every time I look out the window I think of something new I might do."

The decision actually was not made by Bob Kennedy but by his brother and Abraham Ribicoff. Governor Ribicoff had been one of John Kennedy's earliest supporters for the Presidency, and furthermore, he had delivered the state of Connecticut by a whopping majority. Kennedy sought to reward him by naming him Attorney General, but Ribicoff refused the job.

In the first place, Ribicoff said, he wanted a position where he could do something constructive and the Attorney General is always doing something destructive—breaking up trusts, prosecuting criminals, and the like. Besides, he said, the Justice Department's Number One problem of the times was not one for him to handle. "How would it be politically," he asked, "if the Jewish Attorney General of a Catholic President is forcing Negro students into white Protestant schools?" What he wanted, Ribicoff said, was the Secretaryship of Health, Education and Welfare.

Soapy Williams wanted that, too, but Kennedy thought Ribicoff was qualified where Williams was not. Ribicoff was a moderate who would not cause Congress' conservatives to panic when he appeared on Capitol Hill advocating social legislation. Ribicoff was so acceptable to all shades politically that as governor he carried Connecticut's Fairfield County, normally one of the nation's foremost strongholds of Republicanism.

Ribicoff was appointed Secretary of Health, Education and Welfare. That left the Attorney General's position still open. John Kennedy put new pressure on his brother, Bobby, to accept it. Bobby talked to his father, who advised him to take the job. "There'll be a storm at first about nepotism, but it'll soon die down and everyone will forget it if you do a good job," the elder Kennedy said.

Bobby wrestled with the problem—"I changed my mind five times today alone," he told one friend—and then decided. He would accept the appointment. "We'll announce it at midnight so no one will notice it," John Kennedy joked.

The announcement was not made at midnight, but it was made, by purest chance, a few hours after two airliners collided over New York City. The Kennedy appointment did not get nearly the newspaper prominence it might have attracted on another day. Nevertheless, it did not go unnoticed. The Bobby Kennedy appointment drew more critical mail than all of the other appointments combined.

This was a minor surprise because the proposed appointment had passed the trial balloon test. Many of the Kennedy appointments, as a matter of fact, had been tested by trial balloon, partly as he sought to draw out any justifiable objections he might have overlooked and partly because he did not want to diminish his mandate, as small as it was, even before he took office.

A trial balloon works like this: Someone in the Kennedy entourage tips newspaper reporters that Joe Doakes probably will be named Secretary of Commerce. The newspapers print this, and the Kennedy people sit back and watch the reaction. If the proposed appointment is praised or even ignored, they go ahead with it. If the appointment attracts a howl of protest, they simply deny it was ever considered.

At times there were so many trial balloons floating above the Kennedy headquarters you couldn't see the sky. They worked all sorts of ways and served all sorts of purposes. Sometimes the Kennedy people were the targets rather than the dispatchers.

One appointment Kennedy considered was that of Arkansas' Senator William Fulbright as Secretary of State. Fulbright had distinguished himself as chairman of the Senate Foreign Relations Committee and was well liked in Washington. Too, he was in great political distress. He was faced with a re-election campaign in which his opponent was likely to be Governor Orval Faubus, who once again would be beclouding all real issues with puffs of the smoke of racism. But during the crisis over Little Rock's Central High

School, Fulbright had remained discreetly silent, and now he was paying the price. Every time his name was mentioned in the inner circles as possible Secretary of State, Bobby Kennedy snapped, "You can't have a Secretary of State from Little Rock." Finally, a trial balloon was floated to determine how universal was Bobby's feeling. The word went out that Fulbright was all but assured of the job. The protests from Negro and liberal groups were immediate, and Fulbright was dropped from consideration.

Vice President-elect Lyndon Johnson wanted Congressman William Dawson of Illinois to get the job of Postmaster General. Dawson was a special ally of Johnson's mentor, House Speaker Sam Rayburn. From Johnson's friends the tip went out to newspapers that Dawson was about to get the appointment. This seemed to put Kennedy on a special spot. Dawson is a Negro, and if Kennedy rejected the idea once it was publicized, he might appear to be spurning Dawson because of his race. The Kennedy forces were too fleet-footed to be caught, however. Before the idea took hold they convinced Dawson, who is 71, that a younger man would do better in the job. Then Kennedy publicly offered Dawson the job, received Dawson's refusal, and everyone, or almost everyone, was happy again.

There was quite a bit of this hauling and tugging within the ranks of the victorious Kennedy-Johnson ticket, but it produced no permanent bitterness. Kennedy always was spared any serious recrimination by the fact that he had never made any firm promises of patronage during the campaign.

This made the Kennedy search for "the best man" for every job more practical, if not more fruitful, than it might otherwise have been. Once he had exhausted his limited list of acquaintances who might fill jobs, he began interviewing strangers. His Cabinet eventually was composed of "nine strangers and a brother," according to a Washington quip of the moment.

No one man or even one group of men supplied the names from which Kennedy eventually selected his government. But the most important single figure was Robert A. Lovett, a New York banker who had served in both the Roosevelt and Truman administrations. Kennedy's father suggested he talk to Lovett and Kennedy was ecstatic after the first conversation. "At last I've found a disinterested man," he said.

Lovett would not join the administration. Kennedy begged him to take a job, any job, but Lovett insisted that his health wasn't good enough. He was willing, however, to offer Cabinet suggestions, and eventually his nominees were placed in two of the most important jobs.

Lovett suggested that Dean Rusk, the head of the Rockefeller Foundation, might make the ideal Secretary of State and that Robert McNamara, the president of the Ford Motor Company, might be Secretary of Defense. Kennedy began investigating both men. He had never met either.

Rusk had considerable experience in the second and third echelons of the State Department. Kennedy called on Dean Acheson, who had been Secretary of State while Rusk served in the department, and Acheson heaped handsome praise on the prospect. Kennedy called Rusk in for a conference, and they talked for 30 minutes. It was typical of the Kennedy approach: Rusk left the red-brick house in Georgetown assuming he had been eliminated from the running since Kennedy had made no offer. (Rusk telephoned his wife: "I just had my brain picked, but don't worry. We're not going to move.") Yet, four days later, his appointment was announced.

That was easy. McNamara was a little tougher. He was right down Kennedy's alley as Secretary of Defense because he supplied the intellectual tone as a former member of the Harvard faculty and still answered all the hardheaded business needs of the job as the head of Ford. He did not leap at the opportunity, however. He was concerned about his financial problem, for it would be almost impossible for him to invest his Ford earnings in any corporation which did not indirectly, if not directly, cater to the Defense Department. As troops around the world must be supplied with everything from toothpaste to tanks, is there anything the Army does not buy? McNamara also was determined to be no bearer of hollow authority. He made it plain he must select his own subordinates, and, furthermore, he subsequently exercised that authority, even though it meant political embarrassment to the administration.

McNamara talked with Kennedy twice and he talked to the Eisenhower administration's Secretary of Defense, Thomas Gates, before he finally agreed to accept the appointment.

On the other hand, C. Douglas Dillon was not the least bit coy when Kennedy sought him as Secretary of the Treasury. Dillon was a Republican and already in the Eisenhower administration as the Number Two man in the State Department. As Kennedy pressed on in his search for "the best man," he soon decided that he would not be limited by party label. He was even prepared to take Eisenhower people despite their connection with the administration against which he had just campaigned. He knew Dillon slightly, and everyone in Washington whose advice he sought was high in praise of the man. This was especially significant in view of Dillon's personality. He is dour and quiet and isolated, not given to socializing. These people who so lauded him could hardly have been cocktail-party buddies because Dillon didn't have this sort of friend; the praise could only be the result of his work.

It had been obvious that neither President Eisenhower nor Vice President Nixon was interested in providing manpower for the new administration, but nevertheless Pierre Salinger, Kennedy's press secretary, called Dillon and asked if the President-elect might talk to him.

Dillon, once an investment banker in New York, yearned to remain in Washington. He offered to call upon Kennedy immediately, but Kennedy instead insisted that he come to Dillon's house in the interests of secrecy. Reporters were forever watching those who entered and left the Kennedy home.

There was no job tendered during that first conversation. Instead, the trial balloon went soaring up again. No one shot it down, and so Dillon was offered the job of Secretary of Treasury. He talked to Eisenhower and Nixon about it. Dillon now maintains they voiced no objection. They say privately that they could hardly have ordered him to refuse the job but that they nevertheless had made it damn plain they'd rather no member of the Eisenhower administration work for the Kennedys.

At any rate, Dillon took the job. Another Cabinet position was at last filled.

Indebted because of the solid support he received from organized labor, Kennedy was willing to permit the union chiefs to select his Secretary of Labor. This should have been easy, but it wasn't. Although the American Federation of Labor and the CIO long ago merged in fact, they are still very much apart in spirit. The old craft unions of the AFL belong to one clique and the old industral unions of the CIO belong to another. They began to squabble. George Meany, as spiritual leader of the crafts group, wanted a union president, either George Harrison of the railway clerks or Joseph Keenan of the electrical workers, to get the job. The CIO group wanted Arthur Goldberg, the CIO's attorney. Kennedy eventually had to choose, and Goldberg was the choice.

There was similar tugging over the job of Secretary of Agriculture. Governor Orville Freeman of Minnesota wanted the job and Kennedy was indebted to him; Freeman supported Kennedy for the nomination while the state's two Senators, Hubert Humphrey and Eugene McCarthy, were still plumping for Adlai Stevenson. Humphrey, though, was an old Kennedy friend, and he had to be listened to as he objected to Freeman's selection. Humphrey had his own candidate, the president of the Missouri Farmers Association, Fred Heinkel, who, in turn, was prepared to appoint Humphrey's administrative assistant as an undersecretary.

Kennedy strove for compromise and interviewed a number of prospects. But none of the compromises suited him. Heinkel, Kennedy later told friends, couldn't suggest a single solution to a major farm problem. Kennedy called another candidate "too dreary." He said he "couldn't understand" what still another was talking about. It was a circular road. He soon wound up right back where he started, with Freeman.

As time was running out, the Kennedy headquarters pushed on in a spirit of desperation to fill the jobs which simply had to be filled by January 20th. There was no common pattern in the selection. Governor Luther Hodges of North Carolina read in the newspaper that he was being appointed Secretary of Commerce even before anyone ever telephoned to ask if he'd consider the position. J. Edward Day, on the other hand, did not have the remotest idea why he was invited to fly from Los Angeles to meet Kennedy until he was offered the job of Postmaster General ten minutes after his arrival.

Neither learned until later why they were selected. The choice actually was geographical. In each case Kennedy was given a list of acceptable candidates for the position in question, and he chose Hodges because he was from the South and Day because he was from the West, two regions which had not yet supplied a member in what Kennedy wanted to be a national cabinet.

Yet, difficult as it was to choose a Cabinet, this was only the beginning of the monumental chore. To have firm control of his administration, a President must have his men, trusted and trustworthy men, in the assistant secretaryships, the bureau directorships, the hundreds of positions which administer the policies which are determined at the top. In Room 222 of the Democratic National Headquarters in Washington the Kennedy staff pored over dossiers of thousands of nominees and applicants. Any small mistake now might become a major embarrassment to the administration a year or two hence. It was a nerve-wracking job as well as an arduous job.

Kennedy warned his staff against any relaxation of standards in selection of the second-line people. These often are the most dependable men in any administration. For one thing, they are satisfied with the salary and prestige and thus not as likely to resign after two or three years' service, in the fashion of Cabinet members. For another thing, they are closer to the actual workings of their department than the more august Cabinet members.

Sometimes the talent scouts found what they considered to be the ideal man, only to have him rejected. After Kennedy spurned Keenan in favor of Goldberg as Secretary of Labor, he offered to placate Meany by making Keenan an Undersecretary of Defense. This seemed to salve Meany's wounds —and then McNamara refused to accept Keenan. "He has no qualifications for the job," McNamara said. Meany hit the roof. McNamara called on Meany in an effort to cool him down a bit, but to no avail.

As time ran out and political pressures grew, the Kennedy staff did make some slips. Charles Meriwether was appointed head of the Export-Import Bank under pressure from Alabama supporters of the President, and the hard-pressed "talent scouts" made only the most cursory check of Meriwether's background. When he came up for confirmation the White House learned, somewhat to its own chagrin, that he had been the campaign manager for an anti-Semitic racist politician and that he had practically no qualifications for his new job. The Kennedy people rode out the storm, however, and Meriwether was confirmed.

By Inauguration Day, Kennedy had made only 94 appointments of the 5,000 openings which Clifford had listed. But they were the most important 94. They embraced the 80 top positions which Clifford had cited as being of most vital concern.

John Kennedy had formed a government at last.

Chapter Two

THE WHITE HOUSE

JUST AS Kennedy engaged Clark Clifford to chart for him the problems and priorities of forming an administration, so he engaged Richard Neustadt to blueprint a White House organization that would function with the sort of crisp decisiveness that the new President wanted.

There was no doubt in Kennedy's mind about what sort of President he wished to be. He had stated this quite forcefully as he launched his campaign for the nomination: "The President must above all be the Chief Executive in every sense of the word. He must be prepared to exercise the fullest powers of his office—all that are specified and some that are not. . . . He must know when to lead the Congress, when to consult it and when he should act alone. . . . It is the President alone who must make the major decisions of our foreign policy. . . . Even domestically, the President must initiate policies and devise' laws to meet the needs of the nation. And he must be prepared to use all the resources of his office to ensure the enactment of that legislation—even when conflict is the result."

That was what the new President wanted to do—but how to do it? Former President Truman had pointed up the frustrations of the Presidency on the eve of General Eisenhower's inauguration. "He'll sit there," Truman said, "and he'll say, 'Do this! Do that.' And nothing will happen. Poor Ike—it won't be a bit like the Army."

Neustadt, one of Truman's aides in the White House and now a political science professor at Columbia University, wrote a book, *Presidential Power: The Politics of Leadership,* in which he cited Truman's remark and then went on to analyze the powers which the President has, the powers which he does not have, and the powers which he can manufacture from the ingredients of bluster, threat, and persuasion.

Neustadt pointed out how right Truman had been in his complaint that "nothing will happen." Often the President's orders had been blocked somewhere along the line by someone who didn't understand them, someone who didn't know how to execute them, someone who didn't have time to perform them, or even by someone who thought they were wrong and had the fortitude to pigeonhole them.

Kennedy read Neustadt's book. He decided that the author was the man to chart a White House staff which might most effectively avoid these frustrations. The task was to build a White House staff that would give the President a constant access to ideas and suggestions, that would provide the time and authority to follow through on the ideas, and that would nevertheless recognize that there are only 24 hours to a day.

Neustadt started on the theory that the Eisenhower system was exactly wrong. Under the Eisenhower regime the President's only contact was with his Chief of Staff, first Sherman Adams and later Wilton Persons. A large crew of specialists worked under this chief, took their completed work to him, and he, in turn, presented it to the President for acceptance or rejection. The President had no access to the thought or alternatives which went into a given project. No one said, "We kicked around these ten possible solutions to this problem and finally decided on number six." He was told only, "This is the problem and this is our solution. Answer yes or no." As a result the President became a signer of orders rather than a formulater of orders.

The White House today has a much smaller staff than Eisenhower maintained, and its members have direct access to the President. They don't have to filter through the Chief of Staff and they don't have to present tailormade solutions to the problems. This means that the President knows much more about what's going on in the White House. And if he knows what's going on, he can do something about it.

It is all much more informal than it was under Eisenhower. There is not the tendency to assign a job to one staff member and leave it completely in his hands until he reports to the chief. Rather the tendency is for everyone to put in his two-bit's worth in any discussion. This absence of special assignments will inevitably produce jurisdictional feuds among the staff. Kennedy wants this. He thinks it creates a spirit of competition which will draw out a greater variety of ideas. Also, with fewer men around, he thinks things will get done faster. There is not that wait for an idea to filter up through the staff system and then filter back down before it can be put into effect.

The key men in the Kennedy operation are Theodore Sorensen, the special counsel whose job involves the framing of messages, speeches, and the like; Kenneth O'Donnell, the appointments secretary who decides who gets in to see the President and also what papers the President must read; Lawrence O'Brien, who is in charge of Congressional relations and also patronage, a lethal combination; and McGeorge Bundy, who is the foreign relations power through his co-ordination of the State and Defense Departments and through his role as the President's round-the-clock link with the National Security Council.

Also on the top level are Ralph Dungan, who is the man

who funnels work assignments to the staff; Fred Dutton, the President's liaison with his Cabinet members; Jerry Wiesner, the President's science advisor; Dr. W. W. Heller, who forms vital policies as chairman of the President's Council of Economic Advisors; David Bell, the Budget Director; and Pierre Salinger, who as press secretary is the President's link with the outside world.

Perhaps the most sensitive job is that performed by Sorensen. There are things the President *must do*—the signing of bills, the drafting of programs, the making of speeches. Sorensen is the man who paves the way. He drafts the legislative programs, researches and writes the speeches, and talks through the policy which lies behind all of these actions.

Before Franklin Roosevelt's time there was no job like this in the White House. But with FDR came the New Deal, and with the New Deal came an avalanche of new work—the President was delivering more messages to Congress, submitting more legislation, preparing more documents than Presidents had ever done.

The President lumped all this together for Sam Rosenman to do. It turned out to be a good concept. When Truman took office, he eliminated the job, but within six months he had restored it to the White House organization. Eisenhower, in his turn, split up the work among several staff men.

Now the job is one again. It makes Sorensen in a sense the second most powerful man in Washington. It also puts him under the greatest strain. There are a great variety of matters involved, running from economics to foreign affairs to hardheaded politics to national defense to the quips that will lighten the President's next speech. Sorensen must be versed on all of them. He must act on them in the name of the President and this often means in the name of the United

States. There's not much leeway for mistakes and no time for specialization.

Sorensen is the ideal man for such a job. He is a dedicated bookworm who seldom has time for small talk or lunchroom joshing. He was only 32 when he moved into the White House with Kennedy, yet in a way he had been preparing for this position all of his life. His father had been a Republican back home in Lincoln, Nebraska, but a liberal Republican who was devoted to George Norris, who kept the house laden with liberal publications, and who distinguished himself as a fighting state's attorney. The result is Ted: a studious young man, replete with horn-rimmed spectacles and Phi Beta Kappa key, who is probably the most ideologically intense member of the Kennedy staff.

He is not without either a sense of humor or the staff attachment for touch football, yet he has seldom allowed himself room for diversion during his climb through the Federal Security Agency, and the Department of Health, Education and Welfare onto Kennedy's Senate staff. Sorensen has been extremely close to Kennedy since 1953. He did the research work for what became Kennedy's Pulitzer-prize-winning book, *Profiles in Courage,* and he provided much of the push which led Kennedy to seek first the Vice Presidential nomination in 1956 and then the Presidential nomination in 1960.

His chief assistant at the White House is Mike Feldman, who actually draws up the bills which the administration submits to Congress and the executive orders which the President issues.

Sorensen's great authority today is not the boss type of authority but rather the suggestion type. He is not a mover of mountains for the President but rather a man who suggests how the mountain might be moved. In this capacity he becomes the most influential man in the administration on the formation of broad policy.

O'Donnell's authority in the White House is not so much in what he does as what he permits others to do. He is the traffic cop at the door who waves people in or aside as they seek to get the President's ear. But this is not an autocratic performance which goes on daily. It is relatively easy for staff members to get to see the President. The outsiders from the Cabinet and the other branches of the government must filter their requests through O'Donnell, but the President's attitude is to talk to as many persons as he can in a day.

O'Donnell is a former Harvard University football captain who was a college chum of Bobby Kennedy's. He was drafted from his job with a Boston paper manufacturer to help Kennedy campaign for the Senate in 1951. From there he went to Washington as Bobby's administrative assistant on the McClellan Committee, and during the Presidential campaign he directed Kennedy's split-second scheduling, a chore which well prepared him for the appointments secretary role he now holds.

O'Brien's position as Congressional relations man is particularly sensitive because of the many bills Kennedy wants from Congress and because the Congress is so narrowly divided between those who approve Kennedy's program and those who consider it too costly. At the same time, O'Brien is the liaison between the White House and the Democratic National Committee.

This means two things: first, it makes him the political chief of the White House staff; and, second, his authority over patronage leads Congressmen whose votes he solicits to think twice before spurning his pleas.

O'Brien is not, however, the only link between the White House and Congress. The President himself will step in with discreet phone calls when the chips are down. This is not necessarily resented on Capitol Hill. Former Minority Leader Joe Martin once complained during the Eisenhower administration that Republicans in the House got awfully tired of hearing a middleman say, "The chief wants this" or "The chief wants that." They'd like to hear from the chief himself occasionally, Martin maintained.

Like O'Donnell, O'Brien dates back to the first Kennedy campaign for the Senate. He had been in politics in western Massachusetts and was enlisted in the Kennedy army to specialize in that section of the state. He has been a Kennedy man since.

In matters of both national defense and foreign affairs, two inevitably linked interests of the era, McGeorge Bundy is the vital man. Officially, he is the President's "Special Assistant for National Security Affairs." This mouthful of words adds up to a barrelful of responsibilities. Bundy is the man who must make the State and Defense Departments work together for the common foreign policy. He is also executive secretary of the National Security Council and, as such, is the President's eyes and ears on the council.

It is Bundy's job to get the jobs done. He is the expediter, the man who finds out in a hurry what the President needs to know, the man who follows through to make certain the President's orders are being followed. He is, in Neustadt's table of organization, the man who is charged with eliminating those Presidential frustrations in the foreign-military area: It's his job to correct the Truman complaint that "nothing will happen."

Bundy and his aide, W. W. Rostow, replace a good number of Eisenhower men who shared the work which they handle alone. One effect has been to cut down on the staff and committee work of the National Security Council.

Bundy is one of those Kennedy kidnaped from Harvard. He was Dean of Arts and Sciences at the time he was brought into the administration. Before that he had been close to Roosevelt's Secretary of War Henry Stimson and Truman's Secretary of State Dean Acheson. Bundy's father had been Stimson's undersecretary, and Bundy himself co-authored a biography of Stimson. Bundy edited Acheson's papers into a book.

Bundy is the only Republican on the White House staff, and his appointment caused considerable consternation among Boston Democrats. Governor Furcolo called it "incredible." But Bundy has a long history as a battler for liberal causes. He called right-wing editor William F. Buckley, Jr., "a violent, unbalanced, twisted and ignorant young man," and he was a loud opponent of Senator Joe McCarthy.

Under the White House plan which Neustadt set up, each key man has a double job: part of it is a daily-routine type of job and part of it is an occasional answer-the-fire-alarm job. For example, O'Brien is handling the politics and patronage problems on a daily basis and diving into the Congressional fray only when there are administration bills up for consideration. The idea is to give each man a regular job plus a part-time sideline.

Dungan and Dutton are less tied down than most of the staff by their daily jobs. This gives them freedom to take on special assignments. They are the trouble-shooters.

The basic idea is to have each man on the staff assigned to a specific task and yet at the same time not tied down completely as a specialist without interest or knowledge of what everyone else is doing. There is a deliberate overlap of responsibilities so that there will be extra ideas to choose from, extra inspections of each man's work.

There are, however, exceptions to this. At one extreme

Wiesner has only the field of science and Heller has only the field of economics. At the other extreme, Arthur Schlesinger, Jr., has no fixed assignment at all.

The science advisor job is the one Eisenhower administration contribution which has been retained by the Kennedy administration. It is Neustadt's theory that this job will probably grow in proportions and also drift away from the White House physically—across the street to the Executive Office Building, where the Budget Bureau and the Economic Council hold forth.

Heller, a lanky and urbane economist from the University of Minnesota, presides over the Economic Council which also includes James Tobin, a professor from Yale, and Kermit Gordon, who joined the administration from Williams. Their job is to develop both the economic and social programs of the administration. They, for example, formulated the Kennedy anti-recession program which was presented to the Congress in the first weeks of the administration.

Schlesinger, the brilliant Harvard historian who had for some time been a special friend and confidant of the President, is in the White House to handle big problems. What big problems? Any that crop up—foreign or domestic. The idea is that he will take on anything that is too time-consuming for any members of the staff to handle because of their anchor to regular chores.

All of these men work on the inside, behind the big reception room which provides the entry to the offices in the west wing of the White House. But on the other side of this reception room, as the peephole to the inside, sits Pierre Salinger, the President's press secretary.

Like the job of special counsel, the position of press secretary in its modern sense was created during the Roosevelt administration. Under Eisenhower, James Hagerty broadened it from a mere help-the-reporters functionary to a full-scale public relations counsel.

Pierre Salinger, Kennedy's press secretary, does not make public relations policy nearly as much as Hagerty did, but this is because it is not necessary for him to do so. Salinger, like other key members of the staff, has easy access to the President. But, more than that, he has a President who both likes and understands dealing with the press.

Here Kennedy's pre-Presidential friendships are involved. Both the President and his brother, Bobby, were facile handlers of the press in the Senate. This was done by confiding in reporters, by leaking information to them, and by breaking bread with them. It was an unbeatable combination, for in effect it enlisted the reporters on their side.

Salinger, a stoutish pleasant man, brings to his job considerable professional skill. He was a city editor of the *San Francisco Chronicle* and a writer on *Collier's Magazine*. He had been investigating the Teamsters' Union when *Collier's* folded, and Bobby Kennedy invited him to come—and bring his notes—to the McClellan Committee. Salinger was chief investigator of the committee when he moved over to become Kennedy's press secretary during the campaign.

Salinger, assisted by former Negro newspaper editor Andrew Hatcher, operates from a position of strength in that the reporters with whom he must deal for the most part like him and his boss.

All of this organization centers around a single man—the President of the United States. And what about him? What does he do?

In the White House John Kennedy is mostly a listener. He spends hour after hour hearing reports from his Cabinet, his staff, the emissaries from other departments in the government. It is from these talks and the staff work that he makes decisions.

Kennedy works hard at it. His day begins in his office about 8, and it lasts until past dark. Kennedy moves about the White House offices frequently, with agility both mental and physical. The staff is constantly amazed at how much he knows—how much detailed information he carries in his head and how much he is aware of what they are working on and how they're progressing.

Kennedy is the fastest and most frequent mover the White House has seen since Harding. His Secret Service detail is learning to live with this. Coolidge followed the schedule of the day. Roosevelt's movements had to be planned well in advance because he was crippled. Truman began his White House career with an independent streak but soon capitulated to the Secret Service restrictions, mostly because he didn't want the agents in constant panic. Eisenhower was an old Army man who followed a daily routine. But Kennedy pops into movies, into parties, and, unannounced, into friends' living rooms with gay abandon.

Whether it is at a party or in an office conference, he remains with a person only so long as he is gaining something from the conversation; the moment he feels he's milked all he can out of it, there is an unmistakable air of "you're dismissed" about him.

The President has a temper, and when something goes wrong at the White House he will swear like the sailor he was. But the outburst ends quickly and he holds no grudges against his staff. However, he is not so likely to forget when he feels someone has let him down in a political scrap.

He fought very hard, against seemingly insurmountable political odds, to become President. Now he works hard at it and thrives on the labor. It is his life and love.

Chapter Three

THE VICE PRESIDENT

THE MORNING after Kennedy received the Democratic National Convention's nomination for the Presidency, he telephoned Adlai Stevenson. "I'd like to see you," Kennedy said.

"I intended to call upon you," Stevenson replied. "I have a meeting now to thank those who were supporting me. I'll come this afternoon."

"No," said Kennedy with determination in his voice. "I'd like to see you right away. There's something I have to tell you."

Stevenson made it to Kennedy's Biltmore Hotel suite for lunch, and there he was informed that Lyndon Johnson was the nominee's choice as a running mate.

Stevenson was aghast. The bitterness between Johnson and Kennedy was great. They had spared no invective when they discussed one another in private conversations during their duel for the nomination. "Why?" asked Stevenson. "After what you've said about one another?"

Kennedy's eyes turned steely and his voice went flat. "Because I want to win," he said, "and Lyndon can carry the South."

"Because I want to win. . . ." That was Johnson's function as running mate in the campaign, and that is Johnson's primary function as Vice President: To win. In the first instance, it was to win an election. Now it is to win legislation.

After enduring generations of Throttlebottom jokes, the

Vice Presidency was elevated to a position of usefulness by the Eisenhower administration. Richard Nixon was never the good right arm of the President that he pretended to be, but he did emerge from the office's traditional obscurity to be a definite political and ceremonial functionary. Lyndon Johnson is much more than that. Lyndon Johnson is the White House's overseer on Capitol Hill.

The very real estate of the Capitol gives a good idea of how busy a beaver Johnson is. As Senator from Texas he had a five-room office in the Senate Office Building. As Majority Leader of the Senate he had a two-room suite in the Capitol. He retains all of this and, in addition, has taken over the traditional Vice President's room off the Senate Chamber and two small study rooms in the basement of the Capitol. Lyndon Johnson doesn't need all that space to raise Herefords.

As a Senator, Johnson's great forte was organization. He organized the Senate as a whole and then he organized its strategies on the issues as they arose. That remains his function as Vice President. Although the White House maintains its liaison force with Congress, it is Johnson who is the most powerful link.

At the very first caucus of Senate Democrats, it became obvious that Johnson would be in command when the going got rough. Senator Mike Mansfield was elected to succeed Johnson as Majority Leader, but it was agreed that Johnson would preside over the caucus any time he was invited to do so by Mansfield. The invitation will come whenever necessary.

Johnson's power as Senator came from three sources: first, his authority to make the all-important committee assignments; second, his up-to-the-minute knowledge of the political and pork-barrel needs of every Senator; and, third, his ability to divine compromises that save face for all the combatants.

His authority over committees has diminished somewhat in that he no longer actually makes the assignments, although he can still boom a powerful voice in the councils which do. His equipment and ability for horse trading are as strong as ever, perhaps even stronger with his new prestige and new influence in the White House.

There are some who regard this great Johnson power as potentially an irritant rather than a service to the White House. They see Johnson eventually operating a sort of rival Presidency. Those who make such forecasts fail to appreciate either Kennedy's absolute determination to be a strong President or Johnson's totally realistic approach to the limits as well as the breadth of Congressional power.

In addition to his position as overseer of the Congress, Johnson was given two other major assignments as Vice President. The first was Chairman of the President's Committee on Equal Employment Opportunities, a group which combats racial discrimination by holders of government contracts. It replaces two groups which Eisenhower had set up, the Committee on Government Contracts, and the Committee on Government Employment. The new Committee has much broader and more effective powers of enforcement than either of the two previous groups enjoyed, and is likely to become a significant factor in the fight against discriminatory employment practices. The second is Chairman of the Aeronautical and Space Council.

Under Nixon the Government Contracts group did some good, and often quiet, work in persuading contractors to hire without discrimination. Under Johnson the new and more powerful committee continues to pursue this course of persuasion, but will be more flamboyant.

The Space Council was designed to plot long-range goals in space probing and to arbitrate between the rival services and the civilian agencies on space projects. This was almost an inactive organization under the Eisenhower administration, but Johnson will use it often to play upon the imaginations of the American people as they contemplate the science-fiction world of outer space.

In both cases Johnson will continually use his chairmanships to make good propaganda for the administration in general and for Lyndon Johnson in particular.

The world of outer space holds no terrors for this wise and witty man because of his monumental ego. Johnson does not believe in the word "can't." As far as he is concerned, a defeat is only something that teaches you enough to win next time.

This does not mean that Johnson does not deign to seek the advice of his betters. On the contrary, he has a whole gallery of experts on various subjects to whom he goes for consultation frequently. It is partly because of this that Johnson has enjoyed such success in the Senate. He always knows whereof he speaks, even if the words may have been supplied him by someone else.

Clark Clifford, a former Truman assistant who was the man who plotted Kennedy's takeover of the government, is a regular Johnson advisor. Dean Acheson is Johnson's oracle on foreign affairs. Other consultants are a stream of survivors of the Roosevelt era: Benjamin Cohen, Thomas (Tommy the Cork) Corcoran, James H. Rowe, Jr., Abe Fortas, and Mrs. Anna Rosenberg.

The continuing argument always is whether Johnson is a liberal or a conservative. He scoffs at such permanent tags. He once wrote, "I am a liberal, a conservative, a Texan, a taxpayer, a business man, a consumer, a parent, a voter and not as young as I used to be nor as old as I expect to be—and I am all these things in no fixed order."

This seeming absence of a credo actually is Johnson's credo. He believes that each issue should be faced alone, at the time it is pertinent, and that it should be settled for the total good, with no devotion to dogma or label. In the *Texas Quarterly* he wrote on "What I Believe—And Why." He said:

First, I believe every American has something to say and, under our system, a right to an audience.

Second, I believe there is always a national answer to each national problem and, believing this, I do not believe that there are necessarily two sides to every question.

Third, I regard achievement of the full potential of our resources—physical and human—to be the highest purpose of governmental policies, next to the protection of those rights we regard as inalienable.

Fourth, I regard waste as the continuing enemy of our society, and the prevention of waste—of resources, of lives, of opportunity—to be the most pressing responsibilities of our government. . . .

Johnson's tightrope walk between liberalism and conservatism was pinned down mathematically by Americans for Democratic Action. It said that Johnson voted liberal 54 per cent of the time in 1957, 67 per cent in 1958, 58 per cent in 1959, and 67 per cent in 1960. That is a statistic, but going beyond a statistic one finds Johnson's middle road as a compromise—he is always the compromiser—between the two worlds in which he has lived as a politician. He was a resident of Franklin Roosevelt's New Deal world in its heyday, and he is a resident of Texas' conservative oil and gas world.

Johnson became a Roosevelt protégé in the early 1930's.

The young Texan had gone to Washington in 1932 as secretary to Congressman Richard Kleberg, owner of the famous King Ranch, and FDR took a liking to him. In 1935 Johnson was made Texas director of the National Youth Administration, and in 1937, when he was 29, he was elected to the House of Representatives. He has been in the Congress ever since.

Johnson was in tears for hours after Roosevelt died. He told the *New York Times:* "He was like a daddy to me always; he always talked to me just that way. He was the one person I ever knew—anywhere—who was never afraid. Whatever you talked to him about, whatever you asked him for like projects for your home district, there was just one way to figure it with him. I know some of them called it demagoguery; they can call it anything they want but you could be damn sure that the only test he had was this: Was it good for the folks?"

After Roosevelt died Johnson found another daddy, House Speaker Sam Rayburn, who urged Lyndon to switch to the Senate. Johnson had tried and failed in 1941 when he ran second in a 29-man field. He tried again in 1948, and this time he won by 87 votes. The next time he ran he won by 353,000 votes.

Johnson's moderation ceases when he deals with the oil and gas industry. In this instance he has always voted solidly with the big oil interests. He was, as a matter of fact, so valuable to these interests in the Senate that a number of its biggest operators became infuriated with Johnson when he accepted the nomination for Vice President. They didn't want him out of the Senate, no matter how much of a promotion he might get. They wanted him right where he could keep an iron fist on any legislation which the industry might consider detrimental. Thus some of Johnson's biggest boosters of yore poured many dollars into the Republican campaign coffers as much out of a quest for vengeance as out of support for the Nixon-Lodge ticket.

Johnson's power over the Senate—his "sense of the Senate" —has always been admired for its technical proficiency, but both the motives and the results have frequently come under criticism. The Congressional liberals once sought to undermine or diminish the Johnson influence by forming the Democratic Advisory Council to plot strategy; the Council still exists, but Johnson has never recognized it as anything more that a social club. At the time it was formed he wrote Paul Butler, then the party's national chairman, "Legislative processes are already very difficult and the necessity of dealing with an additional committee not created by federal law before taking action would only create delay and confusion."

He said later, "This one-man rule stuff is a myth. I do not know how one can force a Senator to do anything. I have never tried to do so. I have read in the newspapers that I have been unusually persuasive with Senators. I never thought those were accurate reports. Usually, when a Senator wants something done and does not get his way he puts the blame on the leadership. It does not take much courage, I may say, to make the leadership a punching bag."

Johnson does not raise his voice when he says such things. Rather, when he angers, his Texas drawl is apt to get softer and softer.

He is ever the demanding person, demanding from himself and demanding from others. When an assistant says, "They say such-and-such," he'll want to know who "they" are. Myra MacPherson of the *Washington Star* once asked a Johnson staff member just how this master of the ranch treats his domestic servants. "He doesn't treat them any more menially than he does us," was the reply.

Since he first came into national prominence, Kennedy and then his wife have been cited as the nation's fashion plates. But Johnson is every bit as much the clothes horse as his chief. The Johnson suits are all made to order and the silk shirts are all carefully monogrammed. Johnson considers himself one of the world's foremost authorities on the art of knotting a necktie, and he once summoned all the male members of his staff, lined them up, and showed them the right way to do the job.

Johnson's passion for clothes extends to buying for his wife and two daughters. He'll frequently stop his car to buy something he's spotted in a shop window.

Perhaps the best insight into Johnson as a man can come from a study of his political campaigns. They are a mixture of devotion to detail, folksy corn, shrewd maneuvering, and instinctive showmanship. "Watch for Lyndon B. Johnson Flying In by Helicopter with the Musical Bandwagon" is not an unusual election-season billboard in Texas. And if you want to add dancing girls, Lyndon Johnson always has them, too.

Johnson's assignment in the 1960 campaign was to hold the South, and he did this without hypocrisy. His speeches on civil rights have always been a good deal more militant than his voting record and Congressional strategy, but he was not afraid to stand up in the South and cry, "I say to you we will protect the constitutional rights of every living American, regardless of race, religion, or region."

He was full of cornpone when he spoke. It was "God bless you, Culpepper" in Virginia and "I wish I could stay and do a little whittlin' with you" in South Carolina and "Nobody asked Joe Kennedy Jr.'s religion when his plane went down" in Texas.

But behind the corn there was split-second timing and bull's-eye staging. The rostrum had to be exactly 52 inches high when he spoke. The band must blast the first note of "The Yellow Rose of Texas" the very second he finished speaking. The train must pull away from the station at the very syllable of the farewell.

It is this kind of devotion to detail that made Johnson the legislative wizard in the past, and it is this kind of devotion upon which he depends for success in his broader assignment of Vice President. When he reads a newly proposed bill, for example, he goes beyond what is printed on the paper before him. He reads into it the amendments he knows, from the backgrounds and political leanings and local needs of the Congressmen, will be added before the measure actually is considered for passage or rejection on the floor of the House or Senate.

Johnson thinks this way because he was bred into politics. His father was a member of the Texas legislature when Lyndon was born August 27, 1908, at Johnson City, Texas. The legend is that Sam Ealy Johnson rushed from his house at the birth and announced, "A U.S. Senator has just been born."

True or false, that certainly is the story of Lyndon Johnson's life. He had nearly 50 jobs, running from goatherd and janitor to schoolteacher and college president's secretary, as he worked his way through an education. But there was never a second career considered by the tall Texan. What he knows of the world outside politics is generally acquired only for the sake of small talk which will lead to political talk. ("Who's Lana Turner?" he once asked.)

Johnson is a wealthy man today. He has money in oil,

and he owns the big LBJ Ranch just outside Johnson City, Texas, a community of 65 which was founded by his grandfather. His wife, Claudia Alta (who more generally is known as "Lady Bird"), is chairman of the board of the LBJ Company which operates radio and television stations.

That TV ownership is a sore point in Austin. While the television industry in general suffers from a shortage of available channels, two spots on the spectrum assigned to Austin have never been released by the Federal Communications Commission despite numerous applications. The result is a TV monoply for the LBJ Company in Texas' capital city, which also is the seat of the state university.

Johnson has twice made statements which can come back to haunt his ambitions. In 1955 he described the heart attack he suffered as "as bad as a man can have and still live." In 1958 he said, "I don't think anybody from the South will be nominated in my lifetime for President. If so, I don't think he will be elected."

That was before Johnson decided to try for the Presidency in 1960. Today his attitudes have changed. Today he poohpoohs any concern over his health by insisting electrocardiograms show consistently that his heart is in "very good" condition. And today when he decries prejudice he is always careful to warn against prejudice against a region as well as against a color or creed.

For one key to the Johnson Vice Presidency is that Lyndon Johnson still hopes to become President. In 1968, when John Kennedy must retire from office, Johnson will be 60 years old. That's two years younger than Dwight Eisenhower was when he was elected.

Johnson as Vice President is aiming himself toward the White House. He is combatting at every turn the idea that he is a man of a section; he is a man of the nation, he insists.

He is mapping strategy to show himself as a man knowledgeable in international affairs; he already has a genuine friendship with the leaders of many nations, especially in Latin America, and he will press the White House for frequent international assignments during his tenure as Vice President.

And, more than anything else, he is determined to retain the friendship and respect of President Kennedy under any circumstances. That friendship was tested in the first days of the administration when Johnson found himself with not nearly the authority he would have liked in dispensing patronage, but the Vice President held his temper. He does not ever want to gain Kennedy's ire, for that would mean he would lose Kennedy's support.

And Lyndon Johnson still has his eyes aimed at the top.

Chapter Four

THE SECRETARY OF STATE

It's often said that President Kennedy is his own Secretary of State, but a 20-year veteran of the State Department scoffs at this notion. "These people got the wrong idea of the job from the Eisenhower administration," he says. "It's not that Kennedy is his own Secretary of State so much as it is that John Foster Dulles was his own President."

The historic function of the State Department and its chief is not to make policy but to implement it. "The President makes foreign policy," Harry Truman once said. The Kennedy administration simply restored to the department its old assignment and installed an old hand at diplomatic techniques, Dean Rusk, to operate it.

When Dulles was Secretary of State, he thought big and acted big. He dreamed up the government's policies, consulting only a very few trusted advisors, and then he took these packaged policies to the President for rubber-stamp approval. Dulles held all the reins in the department and showed no concern at all for the department's administration. He was bored by its many secondary functions and never concerned himself with any matter until it became a global problem.

Christian Herter succeeded Dulles and took exactly the opposite tack. He was a staff man who passed out the assignments and then presumed the work would be done. He took information to the President, but the policies and decisions were all up to the White House.

Rusk operates on a middle ground between these two approaches. He supplies information in the fashion of Herter and he supplies suggested policies somewhat in the fashion of Dulles, but he assumes that the choice of policy must ultimately come from the White House. That is the responsibility and duty as well as the prerogative of the President, Rusk feels. He once wrote, "The President, *with the aid of his Secretary of State* and the support of the Congress, supplies the leadership in our foreign relations."

This does not mean that the Secretary of State is a figurehead or a paper-shuffling bureaucrat. Dean Acheson wrote that any Secretary of State must have his President's "most intimate and abiding confidence and respect," and in this Rusk concurs.

The big bald man who directs the State Department was recommended to Kennedy as a fine technician, a man who could take American policies and make them work with diplomatic cunning and grace. Rusk was president of the Rockefeller Foundation at the time he was appointed to the Kennedy Cabinet, but before that this Georgia-born Rhodes scholar had spent a number of years in the State Department handling behind the scenes some of the most ticklish problems the nation had encountered.

He played a major role in drawing up the Japanese peace treaty, he had considerable influence in formation of U.S. policies on China and Formosa, and it was he who first pushed the invasion of South Korea toward the United Nations.

Rusk believes that the United States can determine the fate of the world. This country, he says, "is not a raft tossed by the winds and waves of historical forces over which it has little control." The idea that we can only react to the Soviet Union's first move is ridiculous, he maintains. This idea underestimates "the opportunity and the responsibility which flow from our capacity to act and to influence and shape the course of events."

Rusk is especially opposed to summit meetings. He concedes that they will go on, mostly on the urging of our allies, but he insists that "summit diplomacy is to be approached with the wariness with which the prudent physician prescribes a habit-forming drug—a technique to be employed rarely and under the most exceptional circumstances, with rigorous safeguards against its becoming a debilitating or dangerous habit."

Rusk cites these objections to summit meetings:

With the press of other duties, the President can never be as fully briefed, as fully prepared as a full-time negotiator (such as an ambassador or Secretary of State) because he simply doesn't have time to do the necessary homework. And without this full preparation the President is not qualified to make commitments. (Rusk, scoffing at the idea that a summit meeting might achieve broad agreement and leave the details to underlings, quotes General George Marshall: "Don't ask me to agree in principle because that just means we haven't agreed yet.")

When the President is away from the White House for prolonged periods, there's a lot of work that isn't getting done. The idea that the White House travels with the President is foolish, Rusk says. The domestic problems and the Congress don't make the trip, and when the cat's away, goodness knows what game the Republicans might be playing.

The summit meetings produce extra tension, especially personal tension between the two world leaders. A man's personal temper becomes involved. If Kennedy is personally insulted by Khrushchev in a face-to-face meeting, he may instantly do something rash—something which would set the cause of peace back seriously. This is not nearly so likely to happen if Kennedy reads a wordy State Department cable about how Gromyko insulted Rusk.

Diplomacy, to succeed, must be gradual and undramatic. There is always the matter of saving face in the case of a summit meeting. No one knows who won or lost in secret cable exchanges or closed-door foreign minister conferences, but as soon as the summit meeting ends, Rusk says, people ask, "Is our team winning? Did our man throw him for a loss? Who wins the most-valuable-player award?"

Summit meetings raise false hopes. They create, especially in the people of the democracies, the fond idea that the bigshots will settle everything once and for all this time. No one versed in the world's problems thinks this can ever come to pass.

Summit meetings, if continued, will become a cheap political instrument to help bail governments out of domestic crisis. Says Rusk: "Were not some of us just a bit embarrassed when Mr. MacMillan announced a general election almost before the vapor trails of the President's jet had dissolved into British skies? Is the President of the United States to be caught up personally in the difficult task of satisfying General de Gaulle's appetite for grandeur? Can we not anticipate cables from still other quarters reading, 'My government will fall unless you come to see us'?"

No, Dean Rusk is not a believer in summitry, although he is unable to stop it completely as long as our allies and the Soviet Union clamor for such meetings.

But summitry is only one of his problems. It is Dean Rusk's habit to keep a worry list in his desk drawer, a list of the problems about which he must be constantly thinking. Every time he studies the list he finds he has to add another worry or two.

But outside the office he is no gloomy Gus. As a matter of fact, second only to the President himself, Rusk has become the social lion of the administration. He is a big, easygoing man who is friendly with everyone he meets. He does not have the forceful appearance of a Dulles or the sharp-tongued lack of patience of an Acheson.

For this reason he is especially good in facing Congressional committees, a very important asset in a Secretary of State. Much of Acheson's political woes were the result of his curt attitude toward Senators. There was, for example, the time when a questioning Congressman said, "Mr. Secretary, am I wrong in thinking—?"

"Yes, you are absolutely wrong," said Acheson. It got Acheson a big laugh. It also got Acheson a big enemy.

There is none of this in Rusk. He approaches Congressmen with an "I'm just a simple country boy from Georgia" air and gets away with it for all his background as Rhodes scholar, State Department careerist, and Rockefeller Foundation intellectual.

Richard Winslow, a former associate, finds considerable significance in this. "My point is that Rusk strikes me as a man who can work as a simple citizen just as easily as he can on the most complicated international levels," Winslow says. "I think this is because Rusk has a real feeling for the roots of the democratic process rather than for cheap politics. He is a man with deep faith in the processes and he is able to communicate that faith. When he talks people forget all that political wangdang."

Dr. Kenneth Thompson, who worked closest with Rusk at the Rockefeller Foundation, says, "There is another quality I think is important: In any gathering he always seems to be the 'head of the table.' Even in the company of exceptional and distinguished men the dominant figure seems to be Rusk. This is a quality which is lacking in Adlai Stevenson, as much as we admire him.

"Rusk is able to stimulate people, and no matter what happens in the course of a conversation it always flows back to him."

Rusk is especially noted by those with whom he worked as an idea man—"a man of a million ideas," one called him. He has a great penchant for dreaming up problems which won't arrive for ten years and then wondering what solutions we might prepare in advance. Some of Rusk's ideas are bread-and-butter practical, some are fantastically far-fetched, but they're all ideas and they keep flowing forever. Some examples:

When we first faced the Berlin blockade, Rusk said, "Why shouldn't we run an armored train through just to see what'll happen?"

When the UN first set up in New York, Rusk thought there might be 100 members by 1960. (He was off by only one, it turned out.) He wondered what we might do about housing the delegates, showing them how to get around town, how to and where to buy food.

What will happen, Rusk wonders, if precious metals are someday discovered beneath the high seas? Who'll own them? Are the present international laws adequate?

What if we really find a man on Mars, or he finds us first? What'll we say to him? Has anyone ever thought of how to explain our being, our politics, our geography to such a stranger? We're trying to reach the moon. What'll we do when we get there?

Some of the ideas, such as finding an apartment for a UN

delegate, are most mundane. Others, such as arranging a bull session with the man from Mars, are bizarre. But they show Rusk forever anticipating problems and searching for solutions.

Dr. Thompson says, "I've never heard him say of another's argument 'this is wild' or 'this is crazy' or that the fellow with the opposite view isn't worth listening to. Yet he has schooled himself to act. He can make value judgments—say this is good, better, worst. And once he makes a decision he very seldom retreats unless a new set of circumstances arises. I suppose he is somewhat like Jefferson who had a finely honed intellect and yet was capable of acting with a certain ruthlessness, as in the matter of the Louisiana Purchase."

Yet Rusk is not a man without faults. One critic says that Rusk often gets so wrapped up in what he's doing that he'll accomplish the whole job himself and never remember to tell his associates what's been done. Another finds him too willing to accommodate his superiors; there is much of the bureaucrat in Rusk, and he will retreat under fire if that appears to be the correct strategy of the moment.

Rusk has a sense of Indians-chief relationship—again the product of his bureaucratic background. He has an ordered, chart-like concept of how to administrate, and he doesn't like to break away from it.

Some members of the White House staff find Rusk too much the bureaucrat. The White House people are old friends and have an easygoing relationship among themselves; they find it odious when Rusk seems to draw sharp lines of responsibility: He wants them to stay in their bailiwick while he remains in his, each working for the President in his own assigned category.

Rusk thinks orders should pass down echelon by echelon in proper fashion. This doesn't mean he is a snob. He is quite happy to chat with State Department men 20 places below him on the chart, especially when he feels he might stimulate them to thinking or working harder. But when the time comes to pass out an order or an assignment, it won't be delivered in the hall or at the drinking fountain; it'll come through proper channels in the time-honored government way.

Seeing Dean Rusk glide flawlessly through an embassy cocktail party in Washington, it is hard to face up to the fact that this urbane charmer is the product of a "one-horse, two-holer" farm in Woodstock, Georgia. Yet it was there that Rusk was born, one of five children, on February 9, 1909. His father originally was a Presbyterian minister, but had to give up the pulpit because a throat ailment prevented the kind of shouting rural Georgia demanded from its preachers.

Dean's father (the full name is David Dean Rusk) couldn't tolerate the farmer's mean life, however, and moved to Atlanta, equipped with four bags of black-eyed peas, a cured hog, and 60 half-gallon jars of sorghum syrup to feed the family until he could get a civil service job.

He just made it. The maximum age was 45, and the elder Rusk handed in his application ten minutes before the Atlanta office closed on the day before he became 46.

The Rusk boys loved city life. Dean's brother, Parks, now publisher of a Miami Beach newspaper, recalls that Dean was especially enchanted with the fire hydrant in front of the house. It was the first running water he had ever seen.

When Dean was six his father entered him in school. But Dean already knew how to read and so, after one day in the first grade, he demanded that he be promoted to the second. The school permitted him to take an examination and he passed it although, Parks recalls, "he did spell girl g-a-l."

At 12 Dean wrote a paper on what he intended to do with

the next 12 years of his life: finish high school, work for two years for enough money to go to college, graduate from college, and get a Rhodes scholarship. He finished right on schedule, getting a Phi Beta Kappa key along with the diploma at Davidson College in North Carolina.

Dean was a devotee of the Davidson ROTC, and became its captain in his senior year. When he said on his Rhodes scholarship application he wanted to study ways to attain world peace, he was asked how this jibed with his love of the military. Young Rusk didn't pause a moment to produce his answer.

"Look at the eagle on the insignia," he said. "In one claw it clutches arrows and in the other it clutches an olive branch. I'm the olive branch claw," he said, and off to Oxford he went.

Rusk's first job after Oxford was teaching at Mills College in California; there he married one of his students, Virginia Foisie, also a Phi Beta Kappa, in 1940.

He served in the Army during World War II and went to work in the State Department when peace came. By 1947 he was head of the Office of Political Affairs, and two years later Acheson named him Deputy Undersecretary in Charge of Policy Co-ordination.

If that title sounds like a mouthful, the job was a bagful. It was to do everything that no one else was doing—and to keep an eye on all the other guys in the process.

In effect, Rusk was the Number Three man in the State Department, and of the top brass he was the first man to be reached on the Saturday night that North Korea invaded South Korea in 1950. Rusk realized that any action had to be taken quickly. Otherwise within a week the invasion would be successfully completed. Rusk left his dinner party to find Acheson, and together they determined that the matter must be placed in the hands of the UN immediately. Acheson called President Truman, who was in Independence, Missouri, within an hour and a half after Rusk first got the news, and by the next morning the UN was in session, preparing to send a police force to Korea.

As the Korean war dragged on and Republicans demanded that we quit it, Rusk stood up publicly to defend the action he first recommended. "If we run away from it," he said, "the aggressor will learn that there is great profit in crime, that he will not be resisted, and that his victims are weak and can be destroyed at will."

Rusk was chosen over Senator Fulbright as Secretary of State principally because of that taunt that "You can't have a Secretary of State from Little Rock." Yet Rusk is from Georgia. Is there a difference? The answer, of course, is yes.

Because he has never had to run for election in the South, Rusk has been spared that awful requisite of Dixie politicians—the firm stand against integration. But more than that, Rusk has spoken often of the great harm our segregation policies have on our efforts to woo Asian and African nations to the side of the West. Furthermore, it has long been obvious that any racial prejudice Rusk may have learned in his Georgia boyhood was washed away by his education and travel.

When he was in the Army during the war he met Ralph Bunche, who was then attached to the Office of Strategic Services. He invited Bunche to dine at an officers' mess. Bunche pointed out that the mess had an unwritten rule against admitting Negroes.

"We'll change that rule right now," said Rusk, and together they walked into the mess and ate without incident. "That's the kind of a man Rusk is," Bunche said later in recounting the tale.

Rusk had little or no opportunity to choose his top assistants when he became Secretary of State. They were selected for him by Kennedy. As a matter of fact, some of them—notably G. Mennen Williams—were appointed even before Kennedy decided upon Rusk for the top job.

Chester Bowles, who was picked by Kennedy to be the Number Two man in the State Department, actually wanted to be Number One, and he had performed valiant political services for the President during the national convention and the political campaign. But Kennedy's concept of the State Department as a service arm of the White House's foreign policy required a trained technician rather than an idea man, and so Bowles was relegated to the second spot.

Bowles has had a somewhat checkered political career. He quit his family's newspaper, the *Springfield* (Massachusetts) *Republican,* because it opposed the League of Nations. Yet a few years later he was a pioneer member of the isolationist America First Committee. He made a million dollars in his Benton and Bowles advertising agency and was able to retire at 41 to begin a new and again quite non-isolationist career in public service. He served as price administrator under both Roosevelt and Truman, and after one term as governor of Connecticut, he became Ambassador to India.

It was there that he earned his credentials as a foreign-policy expert. Bowles was one of the best ambassadors this nation has ever sent abroad. He worked not simply among the embassy cocktail parties but among the people. His children went to Indian schools and his wife bicycled through Indian streets.

Bowles later ran for the Senate unsuccessfully and the House successfully, and he was both the architect and the construction superintendent of the liberal 1960 Democratic Party platform.

Bowles' confirmation as Undersecretary of State ran into a minor snag over his ideas about Red China. The matter of admitting Red China to the UN is in national affairs very much akin to the matter of school integration in the South. Every Southern official of rank admits privately that school integration is inevitable yet publicly pledges a fight to the death to prevent it. Every national official of rank admits privately that admission of Red China to the UN is inevitable yet publicly pledges a fight to the death to prevent it.

Bowles had written some plain truths in *Foreign Affairs Quarterly* on the subject, and he had to backtrack on these views in order to appear to placate the Senate Foreign Relations Committee, which was weighing his confirmation. This was strictly for the record. Privately almost all, if not all, of those Senators also concede the inevitability of Red China's admission.

In his article Bowles had pointed out that, like it or not, the Peking government "is in firm control of mainland China"; that "any effective disarmament program will ultimately require Peking's participation"; that we can't negotiate with Peking as long as it remains out of the UN; and that we should try to "restore our traditionally friendly ties with the Chinese people on the mainland . . . if it ever becomes practicable."

This is the undercover feeling of the State Department, both on the policy-making and on the careerist level. It has not been the sort of thing the American people as a whole have been willing to hear, but gradually Rusk and Bowles and Adlai Stevenson in the UN—along with the President—will attempt to educate them to the facts of life.

The State Department's economic affairs are now in the hands of George Ball, an old friend of Stevenson and an international lawyer of considerable note. Ball had a good deal of experience in the Lend-Lease Administration; under Rusk he has taken over administration of foreign-aid programs at a time when the United States is changing its role from that of a charitable institution to a banking institution. The concept of foreign aid in the 1960's is quite different from the aid of the 1940's and '50's.

Following policies launched by Douglas Dillon, Ball is taking the position that the rich Western nations—all of them, not just this one—will help the poorer nations hoist themselves to prosperity. The money now is being treated as investment rather than handout.

The Kennedy administration is convinced that the hope for permanent peace lies in the end of want and the control of arms. Just as Ball is in large part charged with working toward the end of want, so John McCloy is assigned to the full-time task of disarmament.

McCloy, a lawyer with long government service, was chairman of the Chase Manhattan Bank at the time of his appointment. He had been an Eisenhower Republican but became discouraged by the administration's foreign-policy failures.

As Assistant Secretary of War, McCloy distinguished himself more as a humanitarian than a warrior. He spurred Secretary Stimson to oppose the Morgenthau plan of reducing defeated Germany to an agricultural state. He urged, without success, that Japan be warned before we dropped the first atomic bomb. He also became somewhat the answer to Senator Joseph McCarthy's historic question, "Who promoted Peress?" McCloy, it turned out, had helped write the War Department order which instructed commanders to ignore a serviceman's politics "unless there is a specific finding that the individual involved has a loyalty to the Communist Party as an organization which overrides his loyalty to the United States."

McCloy's views on his job as the nation's disarmament chief were summed up in one paragraph he wrote: "In my view we must be ready to consider the most far-reaching proposals, including those for total disarmament, universal, enforceable and complete with international control and inspection. Although in the past such plans for peace through disarmament have seemed to some unrealistic and unobtainable, our present perspective encourages a serious study of these and related proposals."

John McCloy got the Russians to put away the artillery once. When he was High Commissioner in postwar Germany he invited his Russian opposite, General Chuikov, to a New Year's party. The general arrived accompanied by a bevy of aides armed to the teeth. McCloy met them at the door and informed them that firearms were hardly necessary at *his* parties. The chagrined Russians dumped their guns into the car outside and entered the house unarmed.

John McCloy did the job on a small scale. Now he's trying to do it on a large scale.

To a large extent, the entire State Department will be motivated by his success or failure.

Chapter Five

THE AMBASSADOR TO THE
UNITED NATIONS

TWO DEFEATS in two quests for the Presidency were a traumatic experience for Adlai Stevenson. The humiliation and heartbreak reduced him from the decisive and firmly oriented man he was as governor to the wavering and vague wanderer he seemed to be after his second loss to General Eisenhower.

Now Adlai Stevenson has a new mission, a mission which some of his friends think is even more suited to his great talents than the Presidency. As the United States Ambassador to the United Nations, Stevenson can concentrate on the urbane wit and incisive thought which is his forte; he'll never have to put on a feathered headdress to become honorary chief of some vote-laden Indian tribe.

There was nothing off-course about the Stevenson who was governor of Illinois before he was hauled kicking and screaming into the national political arena. The newspapermen who covered his office at Springfield say he was a decisive and firm administrator who always knew where he was going. But after the plum of the Presidency was twice dangled before him, and twice snatched away, they felt he changed. A brash and towering ego seemed to replace his confidence. A certain vacillation replaced his decisiveness. A note of pettiness seemed to mar his estimate of others.

"He was," says an old friend, "off the track."

But, this friend continues, Stevenson can very well get back on the track if he does two things: First, he's got to face up to the fact that his ambitions for higher office must die. The UN is as far as he's going to go. He must conquer that ego and make himself comfortable in this job. Second, he must learn to accept Kennedy as President. Even after the election Adlai had a paternal air about Jack. Kennedy was always the Adlai supporter until 1960, and now suddenly it must be the other way around. Adlai must accept the fact that Kennedy is the boss and Stevenson is the subordinate.

There were three schools of thought in Washington when Stevenson was appointed to the UN. One held that he would only last a few months in the job, for his great ego would never permit him to accept blandly the foreign policy made by other men in Washington. Another held that Stevenson was so creative in his thinking that he would lead, not follow, the Kennedy administration in the development of policy.

And the third view was best expressed by a man who has known Stevenson throughout his years of government service. He said, "I think this is the job—not the Presidency—that Stevenson was made for. He always seemed to me to be the special-assistant type. I never saw him happier than when he was working on the UN Preparatory Commission or helping Dulles organize NATO. He seems to want a direct assignment. Once he gets it he is brilliant in carrying it out."

Stevenson accepted the UN Ambassadorship only after he was assured that he would have considerable voice in shaping foreign policy, especially where it concerned the UN. The climax of these discussions came in a three-way telephone conversation between Stevenson, Secretary of State Rusk, and Kennedy—a necessity which, incidentally, Kennedy resented but nevertheless endured in order to secure Stevenson's services. The agreement had to be set down in vague terms, of course, and there are many in Washington who wonder how long it will last. Stevenson and Kennedy basically share the same foreign policy, a policy of exploration and of mediation whenever there is any hope of success. But Kennedy also will listen to the hard never-trust-the-Russians line of Dean Acheson; should he ever be converted to it, he will run afoul of Stevenson. It is Stevenson's contention that we indeed might be able to reach agreements or understandings with the Russians. He feels also that we have become too rooted in outdated positions; for example, he feels that the United States is unnecessarily exposed to military hazard in Berlin and could well negotiate itself out of the danger without "selling the Germans down the river." Some would call this appeasement. Others would concede it as common sense.

Stevenson entered the UN thinking that the organization itself was in peril. He liked to tell how one friend greeted his appointment with "I always knew you were a brave man but I never expected you to go into a house when the roof was caving in." The roof hasn't caved in yet, but Stevenson did indeed enter the UN when it was in its most precarious position since its inception. There was immediate threat from the Communist bloc and there was potential threat from the American people.

The Communists were hammering away at Secretary General Dag Hammarskjold for his actions in the Congo and they were threatening to scuttle the entire concept of the Secretariat, which is the one single force which makes the UN operable.

But the long-range threat came from the American people. The United States had never lost an important vote in the UN nor ever cast a veto. The American people had never felt the sting of a UN censure. But as the new neutralist nations increased the membership, there was growing danger that the tide might some day turn, that the U.S. might well find itself outvoted in the UN. What will the American people do then? Will they demand that we withdraw? Will they want to evict the UN from its New York headquarters?

Stevenson thinks that his predecessor, Henry Cabot Lodge, did a very useful job in making the UN acceptable to the nation, especially that part of the country which clung to isolationism as an attitude even after it had disappeared as a political policy. But at the same time, Stevenson feels, Lodge inadvertently helped the Russians maintain the UN as a forum of invective.

Lodge was proud of the fact that he could answer the Russian attacks in kind and with great speed. He used to boast about the fact that the Russians could assail the United States in the morning and his scathing reply would be on the record in time for the same afternoon newspapers which published the original attack.

Stevenson doesn't like this. For one thing, he doesn't care for the "brutalities of the invective" under any circumstances. For another, he does not like the fast response; he would much prefer a reasoned and detailed exhibition of eloquence after some pause for thought. Then, too, Stevenson feels that these shouting matches should be removed from the UN. There are many ways the United States and Russia can find to screech at one another for domestic and foreign propaganda purposes. There should be one place reserved for reasoned discussion and sham-free negotiation. The UN is obviously that place.

Stevenson feels we face the danger of being outvoted in the UN partly because we have not used the organization as well as we might. To us it has been largely an arena to fight the Russians. It should be used instead, he feels, as a place to make friends, to win over the small neutralist nations with help rather than with braggadocio or self-righteousness. These nations consider themselves too small and too weak to do anything but sit out the East-West struggle. But they would be immensely grateful and perhaps ideologically wooed were we to convert the UN into a sort of welfare agency to which they could turn for help.

The problem is Congress. It has stood steadfastly against handing over funds to the UN for redistribution to needy nations. The attitude of Congress is that it would lose control of the how and where of the spending.

In debate with the Russians, Stevenson feels that the free nations always operate under a handicap. They must start from a reasonable position. The Russians can take any outrageous stand they choose and have no fear that the opposition party back home will make political capital of the unreasonable attitude.

Yet, as discouraging as the picture may appear, the only direction is forward and the only emotion hope. Secretary of State Rusk said, "No world government can arise from the corpse of the UN," and Stevenson adds, "Our experience with fine Soviet promises has been disillusioning but we must leave no stone unturned" in efforts to reach settlements.

Stevenson thinks that Suez was the turning point of the UN. Since then, he wrote in the *New York Times* a few months before his appointment, "The United Nations has taken on a different importance. It is a different organization today from its early years. And it is now, I believe, in a most critical period. Is it overcoming its weaknesses and its limitations? What can it do now? Should we use it, and can we rely on it more than we have?"

The big problem is a willingness to accept the verdicts of the UN. Just as our Congress insists upon holding the purse strings on any foreign-aid program, so the Russians insist upon their by-passing methods, usually in the form of a summit meeting or a U.S.-Russia disarmament conference.

"There is also the fact," Stevenson wrote, "that the United Nations has no money of its own. It has to get its funds from its members, and when they are not interested in a project they will not contribute, as the Soviets have refused to contribute to the care of the Palestine Arab refugees."

The greatest quality Stevenson carried into the United Nations was his conviction that there can be negotiation, successful negotiation, between the East and the West. That is the hope of and for the UN, and any ambassador who did not nurture such a hope would be a messenger boy at best and a hypocrite at worst.

Stevenson's optimism was expressed best in a speech. He said, "I believe many of our stereotypes about the Russians are mistaken. We regard them as undilutedly ideological and constantly plotting world revolution. I don't think they are." He may well revise his charitable assessment now that he has come face to face with the Soviet delegates, but he at least carries an attitude of reasonableness which must permeate any negotiations aimed at success.

The biggest single problem the United States faces in the UN is the admission of Red China. Our allies long ago catalogued our blackball of Red China as a parochial blind spot which must be tolerated but not condoned.

As far back as 1954 Stevenson attacked the issue in his book, *A Call to Greatness*. He wrote, "The point is not necessarily that we should support the admission to the United Nations of China . . . in exchange for [settlements]. The point is that we must not be imprisoned by our own passions, propaganda or pronouncements; we should not tie the hands of our representatives and hobble ourselves in advance to the adversary's advantage, not ours."

That was prophetic. Stevenson became our representative, and at the Congressional hearing assembled to consider his nomination there were those who were ready to tie his hands and hobble him in advance. But Stevenson eluded them deftly. He would not advocate the admission of Red China, he told the Senate committee, but what if we can't do anything about it?

That is the possibility—nay, probability—which the professional diplomats anticipate. The neutral nations which are becoming the balance of power in the UN may vote for the West at times and against it at times, but they will never concede the righteousness of keeping any established government out of the UN.

They share the view which Stevenson expressed in his book *Putting First Things First*. He wrote that "It is clear that no general control of disarmament has any value unless it includes China, and it is difficult to see how China can accept international control when it is not, formally, a member of international society. Moreover, as a member of the United Nations, Communist China, with a quarter of the world's population, would be more accountable toward world opinion than as an outcast."

There is no doubt about Adlai Stevenson's position. There is doubt that he would be permitted to operate from this position while representing the United States in the UN. The domestic political position is at direct odds with the foreign political position. Domestically, our politicians cannot justify to the voters this seeming accolade to Red China. Diplomatically, our ambassadors cannot justify to the allies this unreasonable blackball of Red China. To say that we won't negotiate with China because it is Communist is not enough; after all, we do negotiate with Soviet Russia.

Stevenson did not want to become Ambassador to the UN. When his own Presidential ambitions were doused for presumably the last time in the 1960 Democratic National Convention, his ambition was to become Secretary of State. But by the time Kennedy assigned that job, Stevenson had no hope of getting it. "Too many friends warned me in advance that I wouldn't," he said later.

He was put on the spot by being offered the ambassadorship publicly. Most negotiations for Cabinet positions were discussed in secret and, save for those trial balloons, there were no formal announcements until the man was offered the job and accepted it. With Stevenson it was different. Kennedy stood on the front steps of his Georgetown home in the bitter December cold and revealed to the world that Stevenson was offered the UN position and was now going home to consider it. There was obvious displeasure spread across Kennedy's face as he publicized this bargaining session.

Stevenson eventually based his acceptance on two things. He was sincerely impressed by Dean Rusk both personally and professionally and thus felt this was a man with whom he could work well. And he feared that if he rejected the job he would appear to be a poor sport who would take the Secretaryship of State or nothing.

There are those who see much that is picayune in Stevenson's make-up. He can throw out nasty little barbs about people who should be his staunchest allies, and he can haggle over the most niggling details, as he sometimes did when harassed committeemen were seeking to make his speaking dates during the pre-election campaign.

But when he accepts a job he dives into it with relish, and this he did as soon as he agreed to go to the UN.

The Kennedy administration was scarcely two weeks old when newspaper editors were asking their Washington correspondents how this triumvirate of Kennedy, Rusk, and

Stevenson was getting along. The question was, of course, about two years premature. It was simply too early to tell.

They began with some basic differences. Stevenson, for example, sees no harm in the President's meeting with Khrushchev. Rusk is against this sort of meeting in principle. Kennedy stands in between: He won't meet at the summit solely on Khrushchev's beckon, but at the same time he sees no reason to scamper with fear when such a meeting appears logical.

But, overriding any differences, is a strong feeling Kennedy, Rusk, and Stevenson share: We must maintain open minds and listen to every idea which might advance peace. Each feels he is strong enough not to be contaminated by the other man's suggestions.

Stevenson's personal ego is further fueled by a cult. Two elections and a national convention surely convinced these people that they are a minority even in the Democratic Party, but their ardor has never dimmed. His fan mail averages 100 letters a day, more than that attracted by the average network television program. Most days, there is at least one letter proposing marriage to this man who has been a divorcee for more than a dozen years. He is especially adored by college students of both sexes, who see in him the one leader whose values they can accept.

This devoted claque makes Stevenson a living paradox. Here is a man who on one hand has the results of two national elections to certify rejection and yet on the other hand cannot patronize a public restaurant without being pestered and even mauled by devotees who want his words for inspiration or his handkerchief for a souvenir. Here is a man who on one hand lives a lone and lonely life and yet on the other hand must flee to a farm in rural Illinois for his moments of solitude.

Personally, Stevenson is a thoughtful man. He thinks well beyond the realm of headline problems. Long before there was a crisis in gold reserves he was wondering what the labor-management wage-price spiral would do to our world market and what might be the effects on American society as we change from a nation of producers to a nation of servicers.

Stevenson is also a frugal man. He is not only slow with a buck but he can be a little delayed with a dime, too. He always seems to be hungry, say his friends, and he doesn't care what he eats. His former law partner, Newton Minow, still talks about the unfortunate occasion a few years ago when he had the opportunity to eat some of Stevenson's cooking. The conglomeration of eggs and tomatoes almost completely cured Minow of the eating habit.

Stevenson has been a big hit at the UN. He dines with African delegates who previously saw the U.S. heirarchy only on TV. He established rapport with his Russian counterparts; this guarantees no certain successes; but it does maintain a line of communication. He brought Mrs. Eleanor Roosevelt back into the UN—an excellent public relations move in that she is something of a saint to so many small-nation delegates. But most important Stevenson made it clear that U.S. policy involves compassion for any men who yearn for freedom.

For a decade, Americans of all political stripes shook their heads sadly when contemplating the waste of a talent such as Adlai Stevenson's. Some wanted him as President and some recoiled from the idea, but few wanted to see a man of such intellect drift.

Today he holds one of the more delicate and sensitive jobs this nation can provide. Those talents are meeting a worthy test.

Chapter Six

THE ATTORNEY GENERAL

ROBERT KENNEDY is many men. He is a boyish-looking collegian who blushed and giggled when called upon to read a prostitute's testimony before the Senate Rackets Committee. He is an experience-grizzled political pro who cannily pinpointed each of Richard Nixon's mistakes after the 1960 election campaign. He is a doting father who laboriously lugged a huge stuffed dog all the way from Cincinnati for his children, and he is a vicious scrapper who, his father says, "hates the same way I do."

The Attorney General is a shirtsleeves worker who won't quit until the 14th or 16th hour of the day. He demands that his assistants devote their last ounce of energy to the job at hand, and he demands that they be accurate and well informed as they do. He is a man with a quick temper and a quicker mind. He is slow to forget a rebuff and he is slower to show compassion for an enemy.

Most men with such dedication and ferocity lack a sense of humor or a spirit of recreation. But Bob Kennedy has both. He can even laugh at himself, and wrote gaily of how a building which he was certain was owned by a corrupt union turned out to be the property of the Kennedy family. He romps easily with his eight children and rides horseback alongside his wife frequently.

It was an agonizing decision, not reached until a last-hour pleading, before he agreed to enter his brother's Cabinet. But once the decision was made, Bob Kennedy did not tiptoe into the Attorney General's office. He strode in with a commandant's bluster.

In this era the Attorney General has three main areas of operation—prosecution of crime, furtherance of civil rights, and destruction of trusts. It is crime which interests Kennedy most.

"I think I'd like to be remembered as the guy who broke up the Mafia," he commented to a friend after he decided to become Attorney General. There are some who wonder if Bob Kennedy can even find the Mafia, much less break it up, for the national crime syndicate is a modern complex hidden under a latticework of shrewd lawyers, clever accountants, and seemingly legitimate businessmen.

Bob Kennedy thinks the whole problem has been poor prosecution on the part of the Justice Department. "We are still trying to fight the modern Al Capone with weapons that he used 25 years ago," he wrote. "They simply are not effective."

He sees the problem as increasingly serious because the underworld is continually investing its illegal profits in legal businesses. "Within ten years our whole economy will be drastically affected," Kennedy wrote.

His remedy is co-ordination. He first suggested a nationwide crime intelligence commission, a group which could collect, sift, and disseminate information about the underworld for any prosecution or police agency which needed it. J. Edgar Hoover, head of the FBI and as such now one of Kennedy's subordinates, objected. His official reason was that this was "dangerous to our democratic ideals." There are those in the Justice Department who say Hoover's real objection was pride: He thought that the FBI was doing as much of this kind of co-ordination as was possible, and he certainly wasn't interested in the birth of a rival federal agency which would compete with the FBI for jurisdiction and glory.

Kennedy's point is this: The local police combat the organized underworld only on the local level. The federal authorities frequently lack jurisdiction in the first place, and even when there is jurisdiction, it may be spread among a number of different agencies, the FBI, the Secret Service, the Internal Revenue Service, the Narcotics Bureau, or the Immigration Service, to name a few.

He feels that members of the underworld syndicate should become permanent targets and that every police agency should be linked in the effort to convict them. Perhaps one department cannot prove a charge while the other can.

It is, he feels, a matter of co-ordination. But it also is a matter of incentive and inspiration. A tax agent, for example, is judged and frequently promoted on the number of cases he prosecutes, not on the quality. Obviously he is more interested in piling up 12 small successes in 12 months than in working the entire year on one big case.

Kennedy's plan is not entirely new. Attorney General William Rogers tried something of the sort when he formed the Attorney General's Special Group on Organized Crime. It lasted 15 months. The members said they were treated more like interlopers than like investigators whenever they entered a federal bureau to seek information or co-operation.

The problem of organized crime is emphasized by Kennedy's special interest in it, but he need do nothing to emphasize the problem of civil rights, which will plague him and his successors for some years to come. The South's defiance of the Supreme Court public school desegregation decision has made it obvious that a ruling of law is not enough; the law must be enforced daily and in each hamlet on an individual basis. Here those many men who are Bob Kennedy tend to clash. The man who is a tough and relentless prosecutor is inclined to push obedience to the law with the deliberateness of a steam roller. The man who is a sage and canny politician is inclined to do away with the steam roller and step gingerly through the briers in hip boots.

An old friend says, "Bob Kennedy has no strong feelings about civil rights. He is not for the Negroes and he is not against them. His decisions will be entirely political. But once his mind is made up, he'll stick to it. He won't be talked out of anything."

At the same time that the Kennedys were engrossed in their final fight for the Presidential nomination during the 1960 Democratic National Convention, the platform committee was engrossed in a fight of its own, this one over its civil rights plank. It was past 10 P.M. when the tough plank was adopted; one of its architects immediately buttonholed Bob Kennedy and told him, "You should promise to support this plank to the hilt. You're not getting the Southern delegates anyway and so you have nothing to lose there and plenty to win in the North."

Kennedy thought for a moment and made his decision. "It's a tough plank, eh? All right, we'll support it."

He was asked if he'd care to read it. "No," he said, "we'll support it."

And the next morning, without having paused to learn just what the plank promised, Bob Kennedy pounded the Kennedy caucus with the insistence that "this plank must be passed without a word changed—not a word." He didn't care what it said; he had made the basic political decision, and that's what counted.

It is the hope of the Kennedy administration that considerable civil rights progress can be made by executive order:

integrating the post offices of the South, cutting off federal funds for segregated housing and educational projects, and the like. But in the two principal fields of public school integration and voting rights, the full load will fall on the Attorney General, no matter what laws are passed. President Kennedy pledged special attention to the right of Negroes to vote in the Deep South, and it is here that Bob Kennedy will push hardest throughout his administration.

In the antitrust field, Kennedy promised, "We are going to work constantly." He says he will search not only for "collusion between management and management, but also between management and labor organizations in restraint of trade."

"Anything which puts a company out of business should be investigated and, if possible under the law, prosecuted," he told the Senate Judiciary Committee.

Kennedy has two special interests aside from the major fields of investigation which fall to the Justice Department. One is juvenile delinquency and the other is the high cost of justice. He is studying the possibility of erecting camps on federal lands as recreation and training grounds for both delinquents and potential delinquents. And he'd like to work out means by which a poor man could carry his case to the Supreme Court.

For all his buzzsaw thinking and scrappy spirit, Bob Kennedy nevertheless operates under two clouds and thus he, more than any other Cabinet member, must forever watch his step.

The most obvious problem is that he is the President's brother. If Attorney General Blank should get into trouble and yet be defended by his chief, this would be loyalty. But if Attorney General Kennedy gets into trouble and yet is defended by his chief, that's nepotism.

When Bobby was appointed Attorney General, John Kennedy said, "There have been, of course, members of the same family who have served the government in positions of responsibility. The two Dulles', of course, were both valuable public servants, one in State and the other the head of the Central Intelligence Agency. President Eisenhower and his brother, of course, Milton Eisenhower, served the people of this country in a number of important positions."

This was true, to be sure, but neither Dulles appointed the other and Milton Eisenhower served only in temporary positions on the assignment of Dwight Eisenhower. Furthermore, there were historic precedents in the other direction. George Washington wrote a nephew who asked for a government job that he dared not make an appointment which might be twisted into "a supposed partiality for friends or relations." Woodrow Wilson rejected his own brother as a postmaster after, he wrote, a "struggle against affection and temptation."

But when President Kennedy was reminded that there was no historic precedent for appointing a brother to the Cabinet, he said, "We're going to start one," and he did.

There is more danger from the nation's comedians than from the administration's dissidents in the case of the Bob Kennedy appointment. In time of stress, the "kid brother" jokes on television and in the barrooms could undermine the Attorney General's office far more than any willful cries of nepotism in the halls of Congress.

More serious and more legitimate is the question of whether Bob Kennedy's experience merited his selection as head of the Justice Department. He is but 35 years old, the nation's second youngest Attorney General in history (and the youngest since Richard Rush, 33, served President James Madison in 1814). What's more, he has never practiced law, never prosecuted a case in a courtroom, and, for that matter, never even served an apprenticeship in a law office. He has appeared before only one grand jury in his life.

After graduation from the University of Virginia law school, Bob Kennedy went straight to work for the government. "I never considered anything else," he said. "I never thought of opening a law office in Boston or anywhere." He spent seven months working for the Justice Department and otherwise has worked only as counsel for Congressional committees.

In theory, the Attorney General is the nation's Number One lawyer, and Bob Kennedy carries precious little experience for so imposing a title, but he does not consider this a real problem. "When does the Attorney General ever go into a courtroom?" he asks. "There are many excellent lawyers in the Justice Department to do that. The Attorney General is an administrator."

And going beyond that, he says, the time he might have spent in a law office was devoted instead to investigation and prosecution of the toughest kind of case before Senate committees. This, he feels, is more germane than time he might have spent in a county court. "I would not give up one year of my experience for the chance to practice law somewhere," Kennedy told the Senate Judiciary Committee. "I think the experience of those ten years is invaluable."

As Assistant Attorney General, Kennedy has Byron (Whizzer) White, former Colorado University All-American football star and for a number of years a top-flight lawyer in Denver. As Solicitor General he has Professor Archibald Cox of the Harvard Law School. There, Kennedy maintains, is the law experience. The Attorney General concentrates on leadership.

As campaign manager for his brother, Bob Kennedy concentrated on political leadership. He promised to forgo that facet when he assumed office, but it is, of course, foolish to think that he won't constantly protect the Kennedy and Democratic Party interests. Although the harassing powers of the Attorney General are so great that we like to contemplate a non-political saint in the office, actually there are many precedents for Bobby's position. For one, William Rogers served as Attorney General at the same time he was one of Richard Nixon's closest political advisors.

Bob Kennedy was born November 20, 1925, in Brookline, Massachusetts. He lived for a brief period in New York, attending public school in Bronxville, but his father then moved to London as U.S. Ambassador and Bobby attended successively the Gibbs School in London, Portsmouth Priory in Rhode Island, and Milton Academy in Massachusetts.

He wound up at Harvard, of course, and a part of his heart remains there. He was an end on the football team, and as recently as 1953, while he was employed as a counsel for Senator McCarthy's investigating committee, he sneaked into a dormitory team's line-up to play against Yale.

After he graduated from the University of Virginia law school, Bob first worked for the Justice Department as a junior lawyer and then managed his brother's 1952 Senatorial campaign against Henry Cabot Lodge. In 1953 young Kennedy went to work for McCarthy's committee. "It seemed like the thing to do at the time," he explained quite candidly a few years later.

Bobby soon developed an intense animosity toward Roy Cohn. This was heightened when Cohn threatened to "get" Senator Henry Jackson of Washington, one of brother John's pals, after Jackson ridiculed the anti-Communist psychological warfare plan of Cohn's sidekick, G. David Schine.

One day reporters in the Senate Office Building heard a

murmured argument between Cohn and Kennedy grow into a shouting match and almost a fist fight.

"Do you want to fight now?" Cohn screeched at Kennedy.

Kennedy's arms were laden with books. He snapped, "Don't warn me! Don't try it again, Cohn!"

Kennedy went to McCarthy, told him he thought the committee was headed for "disaster," and then he quit. He was hired by the Hoover Commission investigating the reorganization of government, but the next year he returned to the committee as minority counsel. This was his big break. The senior Senator in the minority was John McClellan of Arkansas, and after the Democrats won the Senate in 1955, McClellan became the committee chairman.

With Kennedy now the chief counsel, the committee first hit pay dirt with the Harold Talbott and Robert T. Ross conflict-of-interest cases. In the process of investigating government contractors, Kennedy learned of their pay-offs to labor union chiefs. He was intrigued by labor-management collusion and went into the subject more deeply. As a result, the Senate set up a special committee, with McClellan in command and Kennedy as counsel, to concentrate on this chicanery.

That made Bobby Kennedy a national figure. He was in the newspapers, he was on television, and he wrote a best-selling book, *The Enemy Within,* on the dirty ore he mined. He and McClellan are, on the surface, exact opposites. McClellan is up from the poverty of the South and spent years in Washington before the Senate seniority system elevated him to anything beyond routine notice. Kennedy comes from the great Kennedy wealth of Massachusetts and he was a national figure by the time he was 30. Yet a close bond grew between them. It was something of a father-son relationship as well as a friendship of equals.

When John Kennedy decided to make his move toward the Presidency, Bobby was ready. He produced from the rackets investigation committee some of the top talent for the campaign, notably Larry O'Donnell and Pierre Salinger. But mostly he produced Bobby Kennedy.

Bobby was the organization man. It was his job to line up the Democratic grass roots teams and put them to work. He did this, and, furthermore, he was always there to prod when they seemed to slacken a mite. He picked the trouble spots and it was he who made the decision on what to do about them. ("We're in trouble in Nebraska and we're in trouble in Illinois, but we don't need Nebraska and we do need Illinois so we'll spend the money in Illinois," he'd say—and that was that.)

There grew a legend that Bobby was the real brains of the outfit, that Jack did what Bobby instructed, and that when and if Jack became President, Bobby would be the "man to see" in Washington. Actually, those closest to the Kennedy camp say this is untrue. Bobby is the brother but the kid brother. He has a lot to say, then and now, but once he's said it—sometimes "shout" is the word—the decision may go for or against him. He is by no means the boss. Neither is he a sulker. During the campaign he would swallow the adverse decisions as though he loved them.

When victory came, Bobby was not ready. He had been going full steam, and then suddenly he was, he thought, at a dead end. With his wife (he married Ethel Shakel, his sister Jean's college roommate, in 1950) he went off to Acapulco to play.

But all play and no work makes Jack's brother a dull boy. He returned to Washington looking for something to do. He found it and he's happily chasing crooks once more.

Chapter Seven

THE SECRETARY OF THE TREASURY

WHEN Clarence Douglas Dillon was appointed Secretary of the Treasury, there were howls from both sides of the political fence. The liberals implied that President Kennedy was traitorous to award the public purse to this product of Wall Street investment banking. The conservatives considered Dillon a turncoat for leaping from the Eisenhower administration and its tight fiscal policies to the Kennedy administration and its free-spending ways.

Both sides were wrong. For all the conservative atmosphere of his Groton, Harvard, and Wall Street background, Douglas Dillon (he hates the "Clarence") has many liberal leanings. He is one of our foremost exponents of foreign aid. He believes in deficit spending. He is for eliminating tax loopholes. He is, in some ways, precious close to being a New Dealer.

Yet at the same time he is undeniably a product of the investment banking world, determined above all to protect the soundness of the dollar and to avoid spending money solely for spending's sake.

At times Dillon appears so thoroughly the liberal that an assistant once asked him, "If you feel this way, why are you a Republican?" Dillon laughed and replied, "I'm from New Jersey, and when the time came for me to make a choice, you had to be a Republican if you were against Boss Hague."

The truth of the matter is that Dillon actually considers himself a government professional, a non-political technician, now, although he first entered the country's service in 1952 in that most crass of all manners, by appointment to an ambassadorship as a reward for political contributions.

It happened like this: President Eisenhower made Dillon Ambassador to France as a pay-off for political and financial support in the 1952 campaign. Dillon did such an outstanding job in Paris that Secretary of State John Foster Dulles brought him to Washington as an undersecretary. And Dillon did so well in that capacity that he became the Number Two man in the department when Christian Herter succeeded Dulles. There is little doubt that Dillon next would have become Secretary of State had Richard Nixon been elected President.

The leap from State to Treasury is, in a sense, the longest in Washington. The two departments are traditional enemies. State is the spender, the believer in paving foreign streets with American dollars. Treasury is the saver, the believer in locking the vault and sleeping on the key.

Yet Dillon is the one man who might successfully make that leap. He was the money expert in the State Department. He gradually created a constant attention to economic as well as political forces in the nations with which we must deal. He favored straight financial aid when he felt this was the need, but he likewise favored making our allies share the costs when they reached the position where they could shoulder some of the burden.

The big hope at State now is that, with Dillon running the Treasury Department, money won't be so hard to wangle because he understands the need for spending. The big hope at Treasury is that Dillon knows where the fat is at State and how its budget can be more effectively monitored.

Dillon is well aware of the constant tug-of-war between the two departments and thinks he can arbitrate it fairly throughout his administration. He was warned, however, that when he joined the Kennedy administration he was risking a more serious tug-of-war, that between his sound-money leanings and the wild ideas which would be pumped from the White House. He replied, "Before I took the job I read everything Kennedy had ever said on fiscal and monetary matters. There is nothing he has ever said that I can object to."

It is true, of course, that Dillon does not agree with every liberal leaning in the Democratic Party's 1960 platform. But he went into the Treasury Department feeling that it was not the entire platform which concerned him, only that part which would deal with his own department.

In many ways he was ahead of the Kennedy campaign on some ideas. Dillon publicly expressed concern over the rate of the nation's economic growth long before Kennedy was seized upon the issue. Dillon was an early bird in seeing the need for new, more realistic, more respectful relations with Latin America. Furthermore, he was not afraid to speak his mind. He chose that bastion of conservatism, the Union League Club of Philadelphia, in which to make a speech warning that we must "identify ourselves with the surging aspirations of Latin American peoples."

The one period in which Dillon may find himself at odds with the White House is during a period of boom. During times of recession there is no argument. Dillon and Kennedy agree that there should be deficit spending, that interest rates should be low, that the pump must be primed, that the dollar must be protected, that taxes must be cut.

But in time of boom Dillon feels that the government should seek to pile up surplus cash and that one way to do this is to hold down on the type of big spending programs which liberals cherish. In this respect he genuinely deserves his otherwise dubious niche as the Cabinet's conservative.

The men who are watching Kennedy and Dillon most

warily during this administration are the defenders of the Federal Reserve Bank. They fear that the bank's powers to set interest rates will be usurped by the administration so the rates can be juggled for political reasons. Both Kennedy and Dillon deny any such ambitions.

There are some in Washington who say that the lean, dour, balding man whom Kennedy selected as Treasury Secretary will deny such ideas when they seem unpopular and then return to them at a more propitious time. They consider him an opportunist. This, they say, accounts for his easy slide from the Eisenhower Republicans to the Kennedy Democrats without a noticeable qualm.

But those who work closest to Dillon insist that this man is not an opportunist but a realist. This could be just an argument of semantics, of course, but the Dillon supporters cite case after case where this realism, or whatever you want to call it, has shown itself in instances where Dillon had nothing personal or political to gain.

When Soviet Minister Mikoyan came to the United States in 1959 to talk trade, he sought to intrigue the American business community with visions of a great new market which would mean great new profits. Dillon, the realist, knew better.

He sounded the warning in a speech in New Orleans: The Russians will make speeches about buying milk for cash, but beware, he said. When they get you behind closed doors they will be after heavy machinery plants on credit. A few weeks later, Dillon had a 90-minute conference with Mikoyan and confirmed his suspicions. Dillon emerged from the meeting and laughed to an aide, "Boy, when you hit 'em where they are, they hurt."

The laugh was not a usual thing with Dillon. Basically, he is a very serious man, a man of much work and little play. He's at his desk at 8:45 in the morning and doesn't leave it until dark. He works Saturdays and Sundays and he seldom takes a vacation.

He is rabid on the subject of homework. He reads thoroughly every report that is sent in to him, and he expects his underlings to know and understand everything the report contains. He has a fantastically accurate memory, partly because he concentrates so thoroughly on the problem of the moment. Sometimes aides will stand uneasily at his desk for ten minutes with "ers" and "ahems" before he looks up from the report he is studying.

He is extremely popular with Congressmen. For one thing, they feel they can believe him. When his department is caught in a blunder he will concede this immediately rather than waste days of rhetoric in an attempt to cover up.

Dillon drives his staff to distraction by his demand for accuracy, particularly in the matter of figures. That's his old bank training, of course. He was on his way to Chicago to make a speech on one occasion when he came across a figure. His brow furrowed and he began figuring on a yellow ruled pad. He labored for 30 minutes and then said, "Aha, just as I thought. It's four-tenths of a percentage point off." He corrected it so he could give the exact figure in his speech.

He cannot be involved with anything that he does not understand thoroughly. He once got aboard a jet at Miami with an assistant and idly asked, "Have you ever been on one of these things before?" The assistant said he hadn't, whereupon Dillon went into a one-hour discourse on jet propulsion and how an airplane flies.

He can do these things because he is such a quick and determined learner. Although Dillon speaks French fluently he doesn't know Spanish and so a top-flight interpreter was assigned to him for the Bogota Conference in 1960. The interpreter sat beside him for two days at every meeting, whispering translations into his ear. "By the third day," she said, "he had such a grasp of the language that he was asking me, 'Doesn't that word mean such-and-such instead of so-and-so?' It was amazing how fast he learned the language."

Dillon has a talent for placating and compromising and he has been a great help in Latin American relations in this respect. There was, for example, the turnabout by Brazil at the Bogota Conference. Brazil was determined to stand up to the United States and it sent as its chief delegate Frederico Augusto Schmidt, who set the tone of his nation's attitude by announcing that "the United States is closer to the moon than it is to Latin America."

Dillon had an aide arrange a private meeting with Schmidt. Dillon was careful to call upon the Brazilian rather than appear to be summoning him to his own suite.

When he arrived Dillon was met by an agitated Schmidt who flailed his arms and shouted, "Mr. Dillon, you don't understand us."

"Perhaps, Mr. Schmidt, it is you who do not understand us," Dillon replied, and patiently he began to analyze the Brazilian complaints one by one. The men parted as friends. The next morning, Schmidt delivered a warm pro-U.S. speech and changed the tone of the entire conference.

Yet, if Dillon shows a genius for compromise, there are some who doubt that this is all to the good. One former co-worker in the State Department said, "He compromises too easily. It seems to be more a case of if you can't lick 'em then join 'em."

This is, in a different guise, the argument over whether Dillon is an opportunist or a realist. A friend said, "You've got to understand his attitude. He will stick to his guns as long as there's a chance of winning, but he is not one to knock his head against a brick wall."

Aside from what may be an overeagerness to compromise, Dillon has had two problems as an administrator. He is unable to delegate authority properly and he is a poor speaker. He is the sort of man who must do everything himself; with an office full of secretaries, he will look up the airline schedule personally when contemplating a trip. His public speeches are peppered with "ers" and "ums" and he is inclined to drone on too long when he is explaining something to an assistant. He comes off best in a press conference or a television panel show, once he gets warmed up to the opportunity to put his ideas across.

Dillon is a product of great wealth. He was born on August 21, 1909, in Geneva while his parents were making the Grand Tour. His father founded the investment banking firm of Dillon, Read, and Company and bought his son a seat on the New York Stock Exchange for $185,000 on the day the youngster graduated cum laude from Harvard. Young Dillon became a vice president of Dillon, Read in 1938 and, except for service as a Navy ensign in the Pacific during World War II, he remained with the firm until he became Eisenhower's Ambassador to France.

The Dillons own an apartment in New York and homes in Far Hills, New Jersey; Dark Harbor, Maine; Hobe Sound, Florida; and on Embassy Row in Washington. Everything about Dillon and his wife, whom he married while he was still at Harvard, exudes wealth, from his expensive suits to her "baby Renoirs," as she calls the miniatures on the walls of the magnificently appointed $150,000 Washington home.

When Congress quibbled at buying ten ornate chandeliers for the new annex to the State Department building, Dillon didn't fret. He simply bought them himself and had them installed in the reception room, where he felt they were needed. They cost him $40,000.

It was as Ambassador to France, however, not as interior decorator and benefactor, that Dillon first made his mark on the State Department. The original appointment was the most routine imaginable and no one, least of all Secretary of State Dulles, expected anything beyond social competence from the soft-spoken balding banker the United States shipped to Paris.

But Dillon was an instantaneous success. For one thing, he polished his already good French to the point where he could carry on detailed and even technical discussions. For another, he was the owner of the Château Haut-Brion, producer of some of France's finest wines. These two factors made him a friend to France.

Actually, the château had been bought by his father as an investment back in 1933, but Dillon used his license as a French landowner to discuss domestic politics with the Parisians. Thus they came to feel they were understood by this lanky American as they had not been understood since the days of Lafayette.

Dillon was the man who broke the long American silence on Algeria to say the United States "sympathized" with France's hopes for a "liberal" settlement of its North African problems. A few hours after he made the speech, the State Department issued a statement saying this represented no change in American policy. But the French considered it a change in that the U.S. had at last recognized that the problem at least existed.

Dillon grew bolder in his speech-making and ran head on into Dulles after Suez. Dulles proudly insisted that it was "moral pressure" from the United States which halted the French and English drive across Suez. Dillon snorted that it was the threat of Russian rockets which halted the hostilities. Dulles fumed and Dillon subsequently was forced to backtrack a bit; he felt, nevertheless, that he had stated the truth, which could not be retracted.

Despite that run-in, Dulles came to realize that the wealthy Ambassador to France was of more consequence than he first realized. He decided to bring Dillon into the State Department in Washington as Deputy Undersecretary of State for Economic Affairs. These facts and figures had always bored Dulles, and he was delighted to have the opportunity to dump them all into the lap of a trained economist and banker.

Dillon was an immediate success. He branched out more and more within the State Department until soon he was known as its "economic czar." Congress was so impressed with his performance that on its own initiative it upgraded him by eliminating the "deputy" from his title.

Eventually Dillon was in command of the entire foreign-aid program, tariffs and trade, the Export-Import bank operations, the U.S. dealings with the International Monetary Fund and the World Bank—in fact, anything that had to do with economics. Furthermore, he was not a behind-the-scenes worker. He made policy speeches and he went to Capitol Hill to face Congressional hearings. "He had such a good grasp of things that he always came across," said one Senator.

Dillon's success has produced a greater emphasis on economics in the State Department. It is partly because of his attitudes, as a matter of fact, that most of the young college graduates now hired by State come equipped with some economic training; with this handwriting on the wall, many of State's old hands now study economics at night.

When Dulles died it was obvious that Herter and Dillon would head the State Department. Eisenhower made Herter Secretary of State and Dillon the Number Two man. But for a good part of the time it was Dillon who actually ran the department.

This is not all to the good. It was Dillon who decided that the United States would lie about the existence of U-2 spy flights when Soviet Premier Khrushchev announced that Francis Powers' plane had been shot down.

In the process, Dillon made one of the most serious mistakes in public relations. He lied to his own underlings. He told them that the U.S. was not using U-2's as spy planes. This led them to bombard the world with denials, fully convinced that they were telling the truth, and leaving the United States no out in the form of a plausible cover story. When the White House reversed Dillon and told the real story of the U-2's, the United States suffered a needless and most damaging embarrassment.

This is all water over the dam now, of course. Dillon now is in Treasury, where his grasp of economic affairs will be put to fruitful use and where his naïveté in cloak-and-dagger matters is of no consequence. His top assistants in the Treasury Department are attorney Henry Fowler and economist-banker Robert V. Roosa.

Fowler, a soft-spoken, silver-haired Virginian who has been in and out of the federal government since 1934, is the administrator and legal expert of the team. Roosa, an economist hired from the Federal Reserve Bank in New York, specializes in monetary affairs.

Roosa in a sense is a living guarantee that Kennedy and Dillon will not scuttle the Federal Reserve Bank. Not only is it his alma mater, but he has written often on the need to keep it independent of the Treasury Department.

Dillon, Roosa, and Fowler all have one thing in common: They early sounded the alarm that the United States' position in the world struggle involved financial dangers. They were paid scant heed until the gold-reserve problem suddenly moved from the technical journals to the front pages in late 1960.

During the Eisenhower administration the Secretary of the Treasury—first George Humphrey and subsequently Robert Anderson—set the administration's monetary and interest policies. The President was only a rubber stamp when, indeed, he was that much. The situation is different under President Kennedy. Now Treasury is administrative and advisory.

Nevertheless, Douglas Dillon holds a sensitive position in the administration, one of the most important, in fact. Second only to the State Department, it is his bailiwick which will determine the success or failure of the Kennedy years.

Chapter Eight

THE SECRETARY OF DEFENSE

THE DEFENSE DEPARTMENT is the biggest business in the nation, and as such it draws the biggest businessmen to operate it. There was Charles Wilson of General Motors and Neil McElroy of Procter and Gamble and now Robert McNamara of the Ford Motor Company.

Except that today there is a difference. McNamara is not at all convinced that the military can be run like an automobile company. He is not at all convinced that "good sound business methods" are what the Defense Department needs. He is not at all convinced that a few sharp directives will right everything that may go wrong within the monstrous Pentagon.

McNamara is aware that he runs a unique establishment, an operation so gigantic that no man nor single group of men can fully understand it. He can only shoot for an end result of an adequate fighting force at something approximating a fair cost.

It is the fair cost which he is best qualified to attain. He has the business reputation, the *Wall Street Journal* said, of "knowing where every buck is spent." It was as a statistician that he rose to the peak of Ford, although he eventually proved himself to be amazingly adept at that unique blend of sociology and psychology which indicates just what people want to buy and why.

McNamara had been president of Ford for only five weeks

when he resigned, giving up $400,000 a year in salary and $1,500,000 in stock for the Defense Secretary's $25,000-a-year. His decision was made neither quickly nor eagerly but almost grudgingly.

Yet once on the job, McNamara dug in with the tenacity which had worn out more than a few subordinates at Ford, and within a week on the job he had established the policies and objectives of his administration.

He was instructed by President Kennedy to bolster the nation's fighting force which, Kennedy was convinced, had often been sacrificed to economy during the eight years of the Eisenhower administration. But, at the same time, McNamara was informed that there were limitations to spending.

McNamara determined first to get his money's worth out of what he had. His first studies convinced him that much Pentagon research was wasteful. He is not against research but, he says, "You must consider not simply the cost, but the ratio of the cost to what you are getting." Put more simply, is it worth the money? A successful missile is worth billions. A successful slingshot is worth nothing.

Within two weeks after he assumed office McNamara installed an office of management and planning, the first in the history of the department. He made it plain that this was no cover for a massive shake-up, to be accomplished once and then forgotten. Actually, McNamara doesn't believe in massive shake-ups. His new department was assigned to study ways of increasing efficiency and decreasing waste on a long-range basis—"We'll look at little offices and little projects as well as big ones," he said, "and we will keep looking, for often you will find something that was proper and efficient when it was set up grows unwieldy and even unnecessary as time goes on."

McNamara is not a slave to the credo of unification. He recognizes the harsh truth that admirals are Navy and generals are Army and no Defense Secretary will force them to betray what they feel is contrary to the best interests of their service. But he told his entire department just what he expected in the way of loyalty:

"My philosophy of management is this: a) during a period of development of policies I expect free and open discussion without regard for anyone's contrary opinion including my own; b) once a decision is reached all members are expected to support it publicly and within the organization; c) this does not mean that they are to hide their true feelings if they are queried by appropriate agencies of Congress; and d) there are ways in which they can report to Congressional agencies any time they have disagreement which they feel seriously impairs their service to their service or country."

One need of the Defense Department, McNamara felt, was faster decisions on the start of new projects. And one reason for the delays of the past, he felt, was that the Defense Secretary wasn't readily available to the contractors for consultation. He is more accessible than his immediate predecessors.

McNamara is a tough man for his new subordinates to figure out. He's always been a tough man to figure. His acquaintances always considered him cool, aloof, humorless, and an intellectual snob. His intimates considered him warm, gregarious, fun-loving, and a downright liberal.

There is certainly nothing dynamic about his appearance. McNamara has a professorial look about him with his rimless spectacles, black hair combed back and parted just left of center, his ready if sometimes mirthless smile, and garb a bit on the somber side.

"He has," says one of his closest associates at Ford, "more

personal integrity than any man I have ever met. I have never seen a guy so completely honest."

As president of Ford, McNamara was entitled, of course, to company cars galore. Yet when he went on a vacation he would rent a car and pay the cost out of his pocket. He never took a hotel suite on the expense account when a single room would do.

His greatest outburst of rage at Ford came when he caught two executives pulling a fast one to circumvent the company rule against overtime. They borrowed two secretaries from a dealer for extra work, and then had the dealer cover up the expense by submitting a bill to Ford for routine repairs on a company car. The amount involved was negligible, but when McNamara caught them at it he fired both executives outright. It was the sneakiness which infuriated him.

McNamara works outrageous hours. He is at his desk by 7:30 in the morning and seldom leaves until after 6:30. He expects his staff to keep the same pace, but he is noted for the personal consideration he shows his people. One of his major concerns in personnel at Ford was the dignity of the individual. He was especially interested in such matters as fair promotions for Negroes and Jews, not a usual concern of top executives, especially in Detroit.

McNamara is a graduate of the Harvard Business School and later taught there. He was strictly an egghead among the businessmen in the automobile industry, but he has always insisted that a man's ability is his only true credential. The chief engineer on the project that eventually produced the Falcon didn't even have an engineering degree. He could do the job and that's all that counted.

The Defense Secretary's idea of fun is mountain climbing. For years he has taken his family to the High Sierras annually, and for this jaunt he goes into rigorous training, donning a sweat suit for early-morning trots before he goes to work. He considers himself wise in the ways of the woods, but once a forest ranger jolted the McNamara family with a little added lore. McNamara had killed a rattlesnake and he was proudly showing the family how to prepare this delicacy for dinner when a ranger happened along to warn him that the rattler had apparently bitten itself in the final thrust and was poisoned through and through.

The McNamara family was considered more than a little odd in Detroit. They eschewed the usual motor royalty suburbs of Grosse Point and Bloomfield Hills to live in the college town of Ann Arbor, some 45 miles away. McNamara drove to and from work every day. This was considered by many to be intellectual snobbishness, but a close friend insists that the entire family genuinely liked the college atmosphere and naturally gravitated to it. McNamara's chief recreation in Ann Arbor was discussion with his faculty friends. "His real thrill in life is exploring his own mind," the friend says. "He especially likes to meet someone he'll find challenging in a conversation."

McNamara also dislikes ostentation, and Detroit is full of it. He wanted more than anything for his daughter, the oldest child, to go to Stanford, but he refused to use his prestige at Ford to get her admitted and also forbade his friends to lend her a helping hand. She made it on her own.

The Defense Secretary likes to say that he is a Republican who sometimes votes the other way. Actually, he believes that his vote is nobody's business. He has never been particularly active in politics, but he has frequently supported Democrats, including Senator Phillip Hart, who was an ally of the then Governor G. Mennen Williams, who in turn was an ally of union leader Walter Reuther. This was heresy among automobile executives in general and downright dangerous at Ford, where Henry Ford II was especially rabid on the subject. But McNamara showed no concern. He supported Kennedy for President.

There is quite a story behind how McNamara went to work for Ford. During World War II he was a member of an Air Force unit known as "stat control." Its job was to maintain control of the enormous flow of matériel and production—to know at all times just who was producing what for whom and when it would be ready and delivered.

When peace came, this group of lawyers, accountants, and statisticians, like all the other temporary soldiers, began worrying about good jobs. Colonel Charles B. Thornton, who was head of the unit, teamed with three others—McNamara was not one of them—and wrote a brochure on how statistical control could be applied to industry. They mailed it to several hundred companies.

They got a few offers, including one from Robert Young's Allegheny Corporation, but one of the quartet, who was a native of Detroit, got a bright idea. He sent a telegram to Henry Ford II, saying the group had "a matter of management significance to discuss with you."

Ford met with them and decided to hire the unit. The group decided it needed ten men and chose McNamara as one of the ten. He was 29 years old at the time.

McNamara soon outdistanced the others. He was "discovered" by T. O. Yntema, chairman of the Ford finance committee, and promoted to assistant general manager of the Ford division. From this there remained only a few steps up to the Presidency.

Something of a McNamara empire grew within the company. There were several hundred bright young chaps who considered themselves McNamara men and who lurked in the halls just for a chance to get a smile or a pat on the back from him. "A couple of kind words from him would last me six months," one of them now recalls.

These were the "ins." There were "outs," too, and they are hardly McNamara fans today. They maintain that he was ruthless with his opposition and that he devoted too much time to cost cutting and not enough to creating. They say he never fully understood sales which, after all, is the ultimate objective of automobile manufacturing.

But McNamara did have many successes. It was he who led Ford to put in safety belts in its cars. It was he who developed the Falcon, and it was he who saved the Thunderbird from financial disaster simply by converting the two-seat car to a four-seater. The safety belt and the advertising campaign which went with it rescued what would have been a disastrous year, for Chevrolet produced a powerful new engine the same season.

McNamara often lectured his subordinates that a man can perform real public service with a large corporation just as he can in government service. He cited the safety-belt program as an example.

His great weapon has always been logic, cold logic rescued from the fires of a burning committee argument and then simply stated. One associate at Ford says, "He would walk into a meeting and through sharp questions gradually pull the meat from the conversation. Soon the answer to the problem seemed so obvious."

He is a great demander of fact, and this is a great help in Defense Department conferences. He has learned that nothing is more overwhelming in Washington than a great recitation of fact.

When a Senate committee was investigating the relationships of automobile manufacturers and their dealers, McNamara was confronted with the charge that Ford had stripped a dealer of his franchise for no justifiable reason. The hearing adjourned at 4 P.M. until the next morning at 9 A.M. Overnight, McNamara had the full history of Ford's relationship with that dealer compiled in Detroit and flown to Washington. By morning he was able to give a staggering soliloquy which refuted the charge.

One of his talents in the automobile industry was forecasting the market. This is an especially difficult art because cars are planned more than five years before they're sold. The public will change moods many times in the interval. But when McNamara saw the design for the Falcon he decided it would sell 600,000 cars the first year and so he ordered production on that basis. The sales department stepped in and told him he was crazy. It could not foresee more than 100,000 sales. The two factions compromised, planning the production of 200,000 Falcons but equipping themselves for 600,000, just in case. The "in case" came. McNamara was right.

In his job of Defense Secretary he has need of somewhat the same talent—not to determine what people will buy five years hence but to choose between various competing designs for a weapon. Which is the one to produce? On these decisions rests the very future of the United States.

In the midst of this high-powered existence McNamara maintains the calm and demeanor of a college professor. For a long time it appeared that this would indeed be his life's career. Born June 9, 1916, in San Francisco, the son of a well-to-do shoe wholesaler, he began teaching at Harvard in 1940 after graduating from the University of California and the Harvard Business School. Only war plucked him from the academic life, and only that telegram the "whiz kids" sent to Henry Ford prevented him from returning to it.

McNamara is persistent in placing his kind of man at his

side in any operation. Not only did he have his claque at Ford, but refused to accept a number of men President Kennedy wanted to place under him in the Defense Department. One was Bobby Kennedy, who subsequently became Attorney General. Bobby considered for a time becoming an Undersecretary of Defense, but McNamara would not put up with the possible squeeze of one Kennedy above him and another below him.

As his Number Two man, McNamara drew Roswell Gilpatric, a Wall Street lawyer with previous Pentagon experience as Undersecretary for Air under President Truman. Part of his job in the Defense Department now is to seek out reorganization possibilities. He helped prepare the Symington Report, which calls for sweeping reforms, but McNamara considers these changes far more radical than justified.

A key man in the new Defense Department structure is Paul Nitze, who carries the title of Assistant Secretary of Defense for International Affairs. Boiled down, this means he is the State Department ambassador to the Defense Department.

Often, these two branches of the government have been so far apart in policies and objectives that they almost needed interpreters. More and more this has become an intolerable situation. Today the two departments are so entwined in policy that they must co-operate to function at all.

McNamara insists on cordial relations between the two historic enemies. "I talked to Dean Rusk about this even before our appointments were announced, and I'll continue to confer with him on co-operation," McNamara said. "It is absolutely necessary that the two departments work together."

This is Nitze's job. He is from the State Department. As former director of State's policy planning staff, it is up to him to interpret for the admirals and generals the needs and objectives of the nation's foreign policy. He has the special chore of Pentagon representative in disarmament talks.

Foreign policy has reached the point where State, Defense, and Treasury are all intimately involved in the same processes. Matters such as foreign aid are involved with the building and maintenance of bases, all under conditions which the State Department must negotiate.

One of the most difficult jobs the Kennedy administration faced in its formative days was the selection of Secretaries for Air, Navy, and Army. The appointment of John Connally, a Texas attorney, as Secretary of the Navy drew special criticism because he had represented oil interests which had received a Navy contract without going through the normal bidding process. However, there was no indication that Connally himself was involved.

Connally had served as an assistant to Secretary of the Navy James Forrestal briefly during World War II and then went on active duty aboard carriers.

Kennedy had trouble getting a Secretary of the Army. His first choice, Thomas J. Watson, Jr., of International Business Machines, wouldn't take the job, and the next choice, Governor Ernest Vandiver of Georgia, had to be passed over because of his segregationist views. The result was the appointment of Elvis J. Stahr, president of the University of West Virginia, who had served as an undersecretary under Truman during the Korean War. Eugene M. Zuckert, a former member of the Atomic Energy Commission and, like McNamara, a former professor at the Harvard Business School, was selected Air Force Secretary on the recommendation of Senator Symington, who once held that job himself.

They are the deputies of McNamara's force. Their assignments are to supervise administration of the respective services. The real boss is McNamara. It is upon his drive that the defense of the nation depends.

Chapter Nine

THE SECRETARY OF LABOR

WITHIN 24 hours after he took the oath as Secretary of Labor, Arthur Goldberg was settling his first major strike, a strike of New York tugboat crews which had been hopelessly dead-locked until he intervened. A few weeks later he was hip deep in the engineers' strike which shut down major U.S. airlines, and this strike, too, was ended as a result of Goldberg's (and President Kennedy's) intervention.

This made Goldberg look extremely good as a master mediator and he is, indeed, a master at this sort of thing. But for the record it must be stated that before Goldberg entered the tugboat negotiations, George Meany, the president of the AFL-CIO, made a few telephone calls to smooth his path.

Goldberg, as Secretary of Labor, can expect such co-opera-tion from the unions. He is their man. But at the same time Goldberg has the respect of many on the management side of the bargaining table. Even conservative Senator Barry Goldwater says, "Arthur is one man I can talk to."

There is a reason. Goldberg is of labor, but he is not labor. Although he had devoted most of his 52 years to working for unions up until he joined President Kennedy's Cabinet, Gold-berg is an attorney whose primary function has been to mediate. "It's always been my feeling that a good labor lawyer is a good mediator, and to be a good mediator you have to see the other fellow's side, too," he says.

As the man almost in the middle, but not quite, Goldberg developed a basic technique in settling disputes. It is the technique which is the basic strike-ending weapon now that he is Secretary of Labor.

Goldberg simply takes the thorniest issue at dispute and postpones it indefinitely, usually for months or even years by referring it to some sort of fact-finding board. Once this is done, both sides are so relieved that they turn almost eagerly to the settling of the secondary issues and thus the strike.

Kennedy's Secretary of Labor went into office convinced that he would be embattled a great deal of his time. He had warned for years about a worsening of labor-management relations in the United States, and he took his oath fully aware that he would bear the brunt of this.

As far back as 1958 he said in a lecture:

> Ten years ago we seemed to be on the road toward achievement of mutual respect and understanding in our major industries; the Wilson-Reuther agreements at General Motors, the Murray-Fairless agreements in steel, and others that could be mentioned, all pointed to an era of maturity in labor-management relations. But in the recent past I see a hardening of attitudes, and retrogression rather than progress in understanding. Management is tougher, unions are tougher, and the results are not good for either side. . . .
>
> Perhaps the change in climate is largely a by-product of our political scene. However successful collective bargaining may appear on the surface in organized industries—and I am, of course, questioning even this—politically, legislatively and philosophically labor and management today stand apart, and the degree of polarization of viewpoints in these areas is far greater than in collective bargaining.

It was from his analysis of the problem that Goldberg has produced what he considers a solution. The difficulty, he feels, is lack of communication. The National Association of Manufacturers and the U.S. Chamber of Commerce go into convention and "unanimously assure themselves that labor is ruining the country," he says. Likewise the labor movement "talks to itself." The two factions may often shout at one another across the bargaining table, but they never talk to one another across the conference table.

It is from this need that Goldberg developed his idea of a permanent labor-management conference which the Kennedy administration is implementing.

This does not mean that labor wants management's prerogatives, Goldberg insists. Although European unions have moved in on management decisions, American labor long ago forswore this idea. It does mean, however, that labor and management will meet without the emotion, the economic pressure, and the got-to-win attitude which necessarily crowd cold logic and honest exchanges during a collective bargaining meeting. The idea is to work out long-range formulas for long-range problems and to equip both labor and management bargaining teams with an accurate estimate of the other side's wants and needs *before* a strike erupts.

For the next years to come Goldberg sees unemployment as a major American problem—not simply unemployment in the sense of people being temporarily out of work during a recession, but long-range unemployment as a result of automation, inadequate old-age pensions, the movements of migratory farm workers, and so on.

Although Goldberg is a firm believer in strengthening the backstop against temporary unemployment, principally by bettering unemployment insurance benefits, he says it is "even more important to eliminate the causes of unemployment." For one thing, he says, "I think, inevitably, we will have to come to a shorter work week in America."

As Secretary of Labor, Goldberg is striving to make both unions and management face up to the problem of automation—and to see each side of the problem.

To the unions he says, "Labor must recognize that automation is necessary and indispensable. . . . It is not generally appreciated that a significant part of our industrial plant in America is antiquated. Economists have estimated that about $95 billion worth of plant equipment is obsolete or rapidly becoming so. Business must accelerate the rate of plant and equipment improvement and replacement. The labor movement should be prepared to support and stimulate proper programs for the rapid replacement of this obsolete equipment."

To management he says, "Business must face the fact that human values must be preserved in an age of automation. We cannot tolerate any repetition of the abuses that took place during the First Industrial Revolution. Business should recognize that we must develop the necessary programs to insure that the benefits of automation do not bring widespread unemployment."

But as the nation girds to face up at last to the modern problem of automation, there remains the obsolete issue of featherbedding. One of President Eisenhower's last official acts was to constitute a commission which he assigned to study the archaic work rules of the railroads. Goldberg utilized this commission to settle the New York tugboat strike by referring its similar work rules problem to the same commission, and as Secretary of Labor he will continue to press for gradual elimination of featherbedding through union-management studies rather than through knock-down-and-drag-out strikes.

This is not as easy as it sounds. For one thing, union and management often genuinely disagree on what constitutes featherbedding. For another, union memberships often refuse to give up featherbed jobs even when their leadership urges them to do so. Newspaper printers of the International Typographers' Union go without many standard union benefits such as sick pay, company-financed hospitalization and pensions, yet continue to set "bogus"—they take advertisements which already have been reproduced automatically and recompose them by hand for no purpose except to make work for the idle. Since unemployment had not been a problem for printers for decades, the union leadership suggested that the membership forgo this unnecessary work in exchange for a major pension plan; the printers voted down the swap 8 to 1 in a national referendum.

The Canadian Pacific and Canadian National Railways produced one formula for elimination of ancient featherbedding practices. They agreed with the union to let the unnecessary jobs die by attrition; there would be no firings for the deadheads, but there would be no replacements for those who quit, retired, or died.

As Secretary of Labor, Goldberg is enforcer of the Landrum-Griffin Act, that law passed in 1958 to fight corruption and dictatorship in unions. At first thought it might be expecting too much for a former labor union lawyer (he made $100,000 a year from the unions and took a cut to $25,000 to join the Cabinet) to police his old employers. But actually Goldberg has been a foe of union corruption for some time. It was he who pushed the AFL-CIO's ethical practices code into being.

"Arthur has a sophisticated tolerance of human frailty," said a former colleague. "If a good-natured union official buys three tickets to the ball game on his expense account, Arthur will wink at that as something not big enough to matter. But when it comes to criminal intent and the underworld and selling out the union membership, he considers that treason and he is as tough as he can be."

You could hardly expect nice-nellyism from a man of Arthur Goldberg's background. He was brought up on Chicago's West Side, one of eight children spawned by a Russian immigrant who delivered produce by horse and wagon. Goldberg's father died when Arthur was eight, and the boy went to work at 12. He worked his way through Northwestern University Law School, graduating first in his class at the age of 21; he began representing labor unions in the middle 1930's and specialized in that practice until he became Secretary of Labor.

As one of labor's top lawyers, he operated an office in Washington and served for years as the CIO's general counsel. There was the common denominator of unionism among his clients, but these were nevertheless vastly divergent men he had to please: tough, luxury-loving David McDonald of the steel workers, jack-in-the-box Walter Reuther of the CIO, intellectual, dedicated David Dubinsky of the ladies' garment workers, and the tough old pro, Meany.

As a labor lawyer, Goldberg was known especially for his ability to seize quickly upon the true issues of negotiation and to state them so that both sides understood completely. He was a master of give and take, and he had a talent for making friends on the other side of the bargaining table. Once in negotiations he found a noted woman lawyer as his opposition and, furthermore, a pretty young girl as the woman's assistant. The first time the young girl brought up a point Goldberg, the old pro, backed down completely. It wasn't that the girl was right; rather, it was that Goldberg knew she would be so flattered that she'd have to lean over backwards to concede his points for the remainder of the negotiations.

Goldberg was especially good at negotiating grievances. "He always made it sound so easy," says a former associate. "He got to the basic issue so quickly and even though he was representing the union he always seemed to be the mediator between the two sides rather than the counsel for one side."

On one occasion Goldberg was called into a snarled grievance dispute between Pan American Airways and the railway clerks union. Goldberg settled the matter so quickly and efficiently that the airline's executive vice president asked him to tarry so they could talk out the whole philosophy of relations between the line and its various unions. On another occasion the president of a steel company telephoned Goldberg and said, "My personnel people and your union people are so hopelessly tied up on a grievance that I'm putting all of them on a plane and sending them to you. You settle it any way you can, Arthur."

Goldberg's job as union attorney was not confined to negotiation of union contracts and grievances. During the 1959 steel strike Goldberg was deeply immersed in negotiations when he was told that the government wanted to buy some property which the union owned in downtown Washington. The General Services Administration was offering $800,000. Goldberg remembered an obscure zoning regulation and used it to show the government the price should be increased $300,000. That hike had extra importance because of the way the extended strike was draining the union's treasury at the time.

Goldberg was a key figure in the merger of the American Federation of Labor and the CIO, but this was one instance when his usually inexhaustible patience was nearly spent. With the principle of merger established and with some factions in the CIO restive enough to secede if necessary, Goldberg was constantly frustrated by the pettiness of the merger negotiators as they wrangled over the manner of dotting each *i* and crossing each *t* in their agreement. One Sunday morning Goldberg got a call from one of the negotiators, who asked Arthur what name the new combine might use.

"Look," he said with little effort to conceal his disgust, "I'm sitting at home reading *The Washington Post and Times-Herald*. Why can't you name the new group the American Federation of Labor and the Congress of Industrial Organizations?"

Nobody had thought of that.

With Goldberg so immersed in the labor movement for the greater part of his life, there was real consternation in industry over his Cabinet appointment, despite his reputation for fairness. Some of his supporters jumped to reply that after all Arthur was a lawyer, not a labor leader, and he could be a fair arbiter as Secretary of Labor.

George Meany was more candid. He said, "He can't separate himself from his own experience, his own background. He can't do a Jekyll and Hyde. His thinking won't change."

That is true. As Secretary of Labor Arthur Goldberg remains a product of the labor movement and deeply sympathetic to it. But he has always been a realist who could see the frailties of the union leaders, and he has not changed in this way either.

He was, for example, a good friend of his Republican predecessor, Stephen Mitchell. As a matter of fact, Mitchell dined at Goldberg's home the Saturday following Goldberg's appointment as Secretary of Labor. The timing was sheer coincidence. Mitchell had been invited to dinner for that night long before Kennedy appointed Goldberg to the Cabinet.

Actually, Goldberg considers Mitchell one of the best Labor Secretaries the nation has ever had. It was Goldberg who arranged for union leaders to give Mitchell a testimonial dinner in the twilight of the Eisenhower administration. This was, incidentally, quite a turnabout; only a few months before Mitchell had been booed at the AFL-CIO convention because of his action against Goldberg's own striking steel workers.

As the realist, Goldberg thinks that people, especially liberals, expect too much from labor unions. He wrote in *Commentary:*

> There is a disturbing number of adherents to the theory that collective bargaining has degenerated into a conspiracy between powerful corporations and powerful unions, at the expense of the public and even of less fortunate workers. I suspect that one of the reasons for this reaction is that these friends of labor originally expected too much from the movement. In the first flush of idealism, they looked upon labor unions as instruments capable of bringing about "the good life" for all our society. Peculiarly enough, I, who have practiced the art of collective bargaining for more than two decades, have never expected the collective bargaining process, or the labor movement alone, to bring about the millennium.

It's always been part of Goldberg's philosophy not to try for the impossible. He has a special knack for finding the possible in the morass of impossibilities which unions and management invariably throw at one another at the start of negotiations.

He is a tall, handsome man with dirty-gray wavy hair and not an excess pound on his frame, although he loves good food. He likes to use his home as a haven for gentile devotees of Jewish cooking. He had a Chicago rabbi devise a special, explanatory Passover service for him, and for years it has been a tradition for the Goldbergs to invite special guests to the family's annual Passover dinner. Monsignor Higgins of the Catholic Welfare Board and Supreme Court Justices Douglas and Black have been among the guests. Secretary of State Dean Rusk was invited to Sunday breakfast at the Goldbergs the week he accepted his Cabinet appointment, and there this urbane internationalist was introduced to bagles and lox.

Goldberg is of labor, but he is a successful lawyer and lives the part in a comfortable home. He likes headwaiters to recognize him and shows special delight when Washington restaurateur Duke Zeibert sends him soup when he's ill. But at the same time Goldberg calls his Labor Department chauffeur "Mr. Johnson" and is such a pal of his barber that they go to ball games together.

Goldberg is a kindly man. His office employees are devoted to him, and when he loses a secretary to marriage she nevertheless remains a family friend for life. He is considered such a good boss that one of his ex-secretaries got a long-distance telephone call of congratulations from California when he was appointed Secretary of Labor, even though she hadn't worked for him for years and her caller knew this.

Goldberg's daughter is married and his son is away at college, so the big house in Washington seems lonely now. His wife is a painter of considerable professional note. She likes to take such things as the off-register proof of a Paris subway map and convert it into a painting which is at once modernistic and yet discernible.

He has considerable wealth, and consequently need not worry about the future when he leaves the Labor Department. But he won't go back to the unions. "Just having someone keep the chair warm for you is not enough," he said at the time of his appointment to the Cabinet. "You have to consider that one career is over."

And when the second career ends? Goldberg's friends say he would like to wind up as a judge in the Court of Appeals or the Supreme Court. Failing that, he would become a law professor.

The man has quite a lot to pass on, for he's learned many tricks. Once he went to the race track with the late Philip Murray. As Murray lost bet after bet he noticed that Goldberg invariably had a ticket to cash after each race.

The reason was soon apparent. Goldberg couldn't lose. He always bought a ticket on every horse.

Chapter Ten

THE SECRETARY OF COMMERCE

LUTHER HODGES brought his own motto into the Commerce Department: "Organize, sell, promote." That is the credo of his administration. That is his theory as to the proper function of the department.

"Our job," he says, "is to do certain necessary services for business and industry and not go throwing roadblocks in the way." As governor of North Carolina he proved an excellent sales manager for the entire state. Now he feels he has been promoted to sales manager for the nation. One of his pet projects is an educational campaign on "How To Export." Too few American businessmen understand the mechanics of marketing overseas, Hodges says.

But the department he administers is something more than a glorified Chamber of Commerce. Hodges has learned to his dismay that it is one of the most illogical conglomerations in the government.

Ever since it was established as a department of Cabinet rank, the tendency has been to dump any new and unclassifiable organization into the Commerce Department. As a result, Commerce shelters such disparate projects as the Patent Office, the Weather Bureau, the Federal Communications Commission, the Bureau of Public Roads, and a myriad of other activities which are placed in the department only to give them a nominal home.

Over the years one Commerce Secretary after another has

learned that these various agencies and bureaus have so little in common that they tend to become completely untamed. There was a period when some of them even dumped the "Department of Commerce" designation from their letterheads in a sort of bureaucratic secession movement.

The Commerce Department is especially difficult to administer because of these varied activities. There are even further complications in that so many of the bureaus must share responsibility and co-operation with other departments. The Weather Bureau needs help from the Air Force. Hodges' export ambitions must be co-ordinated with the Treasury and State Departments. The Bureau of Roads must often operate in concert with the Defense Department.

On top of all this, there is the political climate to consider. The Commerce Department doesn't present any unusual problems under a Republican administration because the Republicans are supposed to be representing business. But the Democrats are ostensibly representatives of the working man, and so the Commerce Secretary draws the thankless task of placating business on the one hand and representing it as a friend in court on the other hand.

Harry Hopkins, only partly because of his health, finally gave up and didn't even enter the Commerce Department building for most of the last year he served as Secretary under Franklin Roosevelt. Charles Sawyer didn't go that far, but he made it plain he was acting only at political gunpoint when he took over operation of the steel mills at Harry Truman's order in 1952.

Yet as unpalatable as it appears, the Commerce Department constantly must be defended as a besieged bastion by its Secretary. Some government reorganizer is always attempting to chip away its gems for transport somewhere else. Hodges no sooner took the oath of office than he began a fight to prevent formation of a new Department of Transportation, a department which would shear from Commerce its maritime and public roads divisions and perhaps the Weather Bureau as well. Aviation already had been taken from Commerce as a forerunner of this plan.

Hodges is exactly the man to wage this sort of defensive battle. And, going beyond that, Hodges is exactly the man to serve the Kennedy administration as Secretary of Commerce in all the distasteful and illogical tasks the job embraces.

He does not fit in with the "New Frontier" crowd in age, background, or ideology. The Kennedy men are in their 30's and 40's, are well-bred, urbane and liberal sophisticates. Hodges went into the cabinet at 62, rose from the grubbiest poverty, and is far more conservative than, for example, investment banker Douglas Dillon. The more brash of the Kennedy men might even call Hodges not simply a conservative but a reactionary.

He has made no secret of his distaste for racial integration. He is a supporter of the anti-union "right to work" laws. He would have had a difficult time gaining re-election in North Carolina, but that is academic because the state has a law which prevents the governor from succeeding himself. Hodges was not a man of the people.

Yet he will do a job that he feels must be done and do it well. For all his antipathy to integration, he made North Carolina a model of peaceful compliance with the Supreme Court public school decision, if one is willing to accept the strict limitations of token integration as a reasonable start. The few Negroes who entered North Carolina public schools were protected from violence and boycott; their communities were spared the furor of Little Rock, Clinton, and New Orleans.

Hodges merits much of the credit for this. "My job, by

speech and attitude, was to lead and think through the thing,"
he said later. And he feels that the accomplishment was far
beyond the placing of a few Negroes in white schools. "From
the standpoint of the reputation of our state for moderation,
what little leadership I gave, gave us a thrust forward. Compared to other states we have an image that is priceless, that
can't be bought."

Here the businessman speaks. Hodges knew that racial
tension hurts business. Arkansas' program to lure industry
into the state was a whopping success until the riots of Little
Rock, and then it collapsed. He convinced the businessmen
of North Carolina that they must support him in integration
as a means of helping themselves, and this in large measure
accounts for his success. The businessmen of Winston-Salem,
for example, quietly let the word get out that anyone involved
in racial violence would be jobless for a long time. There was
no violence.

Hodges was so certain he had discovered the right formula
that he tried to rescue Governor Faubus from the predica-
ment of Little Rock. Together with other Southern governors,
Hodges drew up a manifesto which would have permitted
Faubus to bow to President Eisenhower, but gracefully, with
much saving of face. Hodges telephoned Faubus and read
him the peace pact.

He recalls, "I said, 'Orval, is what we've got here all right?
It gives you a good out. It takes care of the situation and it
does what we want for America.'

"He said, 'It is all right. Just for the record send it straight
wire so that I can send you a wire back for the record saying
it's all right.' Faubus has never talked to us about it since that
time, never sent the wire, refused to take a telephone call for
hours and hours."

Hodges has much Negro support in his home state, but

not for his integration efforts. Actually, Negro leaders think that the very success he had in token integration proves he could have gone far beyond the point that he did. However, his work in giving North Carolina a minimum-wage law benefited the Negroes more immediately than school integration, and for that reason the state National Association for the Advancement of Colored People's chairman, Curtis P. Meadows, calls him a "pretty good governor."

Organized labor has no such fond recollection. It considers him downright anti-union. Under Hodges North Carolina installed a right-to-work law, and Hodges insists it has done well. He has promised as Secretary of Commerce to fight any revisions of the Taft-Hartley Act, especially that part of it which specifically authorizes state right-to-work legislation.

W. Millard Barbee, the president of the North Carolina AFL-CIO, considers Hodges a very tough anti-unionist. "The way he feels about unions shows me his stature, which is very small," Barbee told the *Washington Star*. It should be added that there is an old personal feud smoldering between the two men. Hodges wrote Barbee a letter telling him that he was *persona non grata* in the governor's office.

The fact remains, however, that Hodges criticized President Eisenhower for sending troops to Little Rock and to the Caribbean (when Vice President Nixon was attacked in Nicaragua), yet sent in his own National Guard during a textile strike at Henderson, North Carolina. Hodges maintains he did so to halt violence. Labor maintains he did so to break the union. Both appear to be correct.

At the same time, Hodges induced the state legislature to cut corporation taxes. The state's revenue loss was not nearly so great as expected, but it did exceed $3,000,000 a year. Hodges thinks eventually this loss will become a profit as new industry is attracted to North Carolina by a more equitable tax structure.

The gray-haired Secretary of Commerce is a tough man to cross. Even his friends are apt to concede that he is "vindictive" or "vain" or "opinionated." He is not apt to be charitable about another's shortcomings. Once someone suggested that an official noted for his long-windedness be asked advice about an issue in doubt.

"No," snapped Hodges. "Ask him the time of day and he'll tell you how to make a watch."

His staff is inclined to be fearful of him. He wants everything done quickly, and yet he tolerates no slipshod work. He is the boss, and a stern boss, at all times.

Hodges rose to riches from the bottom. He was born March 9, 1898, in an honest-to-gosh log cabin which his father built in Virginia, just across the state line from Leaksville, North Carolina. As a child young Hodges, the eighth of nine children, went to work for 50 cents a day in the textile mills. A Presbyterian minister took a liking to the boy and pounded into him the idea that he could "be anything in this life that you set your heart on" if only he acquired an education.

When Luther told his father he wanted to go to college, the old man, a tenant farmer, hit the roof at such fancy ideas. What's more, the foreman at the textile plant scoffed, "Why waste your time with schoolin'? In a few years you can make a dollar a day here."

But the boy persisted, and a married sister took him into her home to help. He got a job as a newsboy on the railroad. This required a uniform which cost 12 dollars, 12 dollars that Luther Hodges never hoped to have. His sister solved that. She sewed brass buttons on his only blue serge suit. It was double-breasted. When he worked, he buttoned the side that showed the brass buttons; when he went to church, he buttoned the side that showed regular buttons.

Luther Hodges made it through college, his own University of North Carolina, and then went to work as a stock boy in Fieldcrest Mills, a subsidiary of Marshall Field and Company. By the 1930's he was in charge of the company's 29 mills and in 1940 he became a vice president of the firm. This meant he had to move to New York, but Hodges wasn't fazed a bit. Manhattan didn't take the country out of the boy. Hodges lived in New York just as he did in North Carolina, concentrating his outside interests in the Methodist Church and the Rotary Club.

He got a touch of government service during World War II as textile advisor to the Office of Price Administration, and that gave him ideas. At 52 he retired and decided to go into politics. He was wealthy enough not to have to worry about money (he owns Coca-Cola interests in South America, some Howard Johnson restaurant franchises, and until recently considerable oil stock), so all he needed was an idea. A friend suggested he run for lieutenant governor of North Carolina.

Hodges remembers the exact moment his campaigning began. It was in a little restaurant in the eastern part of the state.

"I was in a sweat about it," he says. "I didn't know exactly what to do. I had these little cards saying, 'Vote for Hodges for Lieutenant Governor.' I stopped in this little place for breakfast. It cost 65 cents. I went up to the cashier, paid her and handed a card quickly. My hands were sweaty I was so scared.

"I said, 'I'm Luther Hodges and I'm running for lieutenant governor and I wish you'd vote for me.' I was saying all this as I practically ran out the door.

"She said, 'I'm for you because you ain't in Raleigh or

Washington now.' That was her total statement. I started from there."

Hodges was so conscientious that he had a peculiar contract with the company he hired to place his campaign posters on roadside trees and telephone poles. The company not only had to tack them up, but it had to take them down the day after election. He had abhorred the ugliness of outdated signs put up by others and he didn't intend to deface his state any more than he could help.

There were four men in the race, and every professional politician assumed that the amateur Hodges would run fourth. Instead he ran first.

He found that when he got to Raleigh he didn't have much to do. Governor William B. Umstead didn't like him and made it plain that, as far as he was concerned, Hodges could go home and accept his paychecks by mail.

But Hodges persisted in teaching himself how the state government operated. He read books and reports and pamphlets. He personally attended board and commission meetings. He became an expert on the office of governor, and a good thing, too. On November 7, 1954, Umstead died and Hodges became governor without warning.

In 1956 he ran for the office on his own. His supporters chipped in $40,000 as a campaign fund. After Hodges won the election easily, he found he had $10,000 remaining in the fund. In an action unprecedented in North Carolina politics, he refunded 25 per cent of each campaign contribution he had received.

As governor he gave North Carolina a truly business administration. The voters are often promised such an administration, but almost always politics captures the businessman governor rather than vice versa. Hodges was the exception.

His attitude frequently got him in hot water, to be sure. For one thing, he refused to look for a party label when making appointments to key jobs. Once he was asked if a new appointee was a Democrat. "My gosh, I forgot to ask him," Hodges stammered. Another time he infuriated the party regulars by not only awarding a key position to an Eisenhower supporter but adding, "I wish I had a dozen like him." When a conference of Democratic leaders called him to task for his attitude, Hodges bluntly told them that of course he'd favor a Democrat for any job—if the man was as well qualified as his Republican rival.

But while he was unorthodox, he had learned well the wiles which a North Carolina governor must possess. Since the state's chief executive cannot succeed himself and lacks the veto power, he must wield power largely through the administering of funds. The roads and the other state projects go first to the faithful and last, if even then, to the renegades.

At the same time that Hodges was engaged in these complex maneuvers, he was looking after the little things, too. He often walked the four blocks from the executive mansion to the capitol. On the way he'd pick up the paper littering the sidewalks. Finally, he became incensed at the civic carelessness and launched a gigantic litterbug campaign which eventually saved the state $50,000 a year in refuse collection.

But Hodges' greatest contribution to North Carolina was the importation of industry. When he took over as governor, the state, as most Southern states, suffered from the imbalance of agriculture and industry. North Carolina had the nation's largest farm population, and these farmers mostly suffered unending hardship on small, antiquated, and consequently woefully unprofitable plots. What little industry the state did have was bunched in ten of the state's 100 counties.

Hodges organized the businessmen of North Carolina to seek new plants. He had the individual counties form boards which plumped for tax aids and even free buildings for companies which would move into the state. He led safaris of businessmen—who paid their own expenses—to the eastern cities and to Chicago to sell manufacturing concerns on the advantages of North Carolina.

He even posed in his underwear for a national magazine's picture layout about manufacturing in North Carolina. His wife became quite indignant when she saw the photo of the governor in shorts stamped, "Made in N.C.," but Hodges said, "If it'll do the state any good, I'm for it."

He established a Small Business Development Corporation to lend money to manufacturers for longer periods than the commercial banks would allow. He organized the Research Triangle on 4,500 acres between Raleigh, Durham, and Chapel Hill to specialize in business research.

He was ever the salesman. He raised $1,500,000 in less than three months for the Research Triangle. He raised $73,000 from foundations to finance a State Bar Association survey of the North Carolina judicial system. When he sent a friend on a special mission and the friend asked, "What about my expenses?" Hodges snapped, "Use your own money" and got away with it.

During his term as governor Hodges attracted into the state new and expanded industry valued at more than a billion dollars. This meant 138,000 new jobs, with a payroll of $500,000 a year.

Hodges' labor union critics say this is not completely a success story. They say that too often these are fly-by-night operators cashing in on the tax advantages and the rent-free plants. They say, too, that the principal attraction is non-union labor and that any NLRB election sends these men back from whence they came.

The fact remains, however, that Hodges is a promoter of business and this is his mission as Secretary of Commerce. "Making money," he says, "is the simplest thing I ever did." He aims to show the entire nation how.

Chapter Eleven

THE SECRETARY OF AGRICULTURE

THE SECRETARY OF AGRICULTURE is a city-bred intellectual, the son of a haberdasher, who distinguished himself chiefly as a buzz-saw administrator and a fighter for liberal ideals.

But Orville Lothrop Freeman is not at a loss as he performs the Kennedy administration's most thankless job. He was for three terms governor of Minnesota, and no man can fill that position and not become conversant with farmers and their problems.

Freeman went into the Department of Agriculture determined to fight for his constituents with all the stubbornness that made him both famous and infamous during his terms as governor. "Farmers have been subsidizing consumers rather than the other way around," he told the *Farm Journal.* "Our farmers have done a greater job of production than any other part of our society. Consumers in this country work less for their daily bread than do people anywhere in the world. One of my jobs will be to help people understand this."

Freeman did not want to become Secretary of Agriculture, and furthermore neither his friends nor his enemies wanted him to get the job. His friends realized that the "unsolvable problems" (as one put it) of American agriculture can only dig a grave for the politician who becomes embroiled in them. His enemies were convinced that his scorn of compromise would lead him to make bad things worse.

But Freeman had to become Secretary of Agriculture. For one thing, he was defeated in his bid for a fourth term as governor. For another, President Kennedy could find no other acceptable man. The Secretary of Agriculture, for political reasons, had to be from the Midwest (for that was a Kennedy campaign promise) and a liberal (for that is the mood of the administration). Thus Freeman, who wanted the cocktails and cookies of the State Department, got instead the dirt and despair of the Agriculture Department.

The nation's farm problem is horrendous. Although the United States has been spending nearly four billion dollars a year to support prices, when Freeman took office farmers' income was down 14 per cent over the last ten years. At the same time, farm surplus stocks were continuing to mount and the disgusted farmers themselves were going into new occupations at the rate of one every five minutes.

A task force report prepared for President Kennedy said:

> Under present Federal agricultural programs, with average weather, total farm output probably will continue to rise at a faster rate than market outlets. This means that with no change in programs, the United States will continue to accumulate surpluses. The net cost of Federal farm price supports, storage and disposal programs probably will remain in the range of recent years— two to four billion dollars.

> The overproduction of grain is the center of the farm surplus problem—affecting most of American agriculture directly or indirectly. . . . If the grain surplus is not brought under control soon it will spill rapidly into the livestock industries, resulting in expansion of meat, dairy products and poultry products and sharply lower prices and net incomes for the producers of these products.

Can *anything* be done? Freeman went into office thinking that there are ways of diminishing the problem if not solving it. "Fundamentally," he said, "there needs to be some acreage taken out of production." This means the soil bank—the paying of farmers by the government to let chunks of their land sit idle.

Freeman's basic theories are exactly the opposite of those held by his predecessor, Ezra Taft Benson. As Secretary of Agriculture Benson worked for a completely free market for farm products. Freeman is shooting toward a thoroughly controlled market. It is his contention that, if the farmers want artificially propped prices, they must accept the odious federal controls which permit the government to maintain those prices. He feels that too often the farmers have wanted to have their cake and eat it too: They wanted the government to mail the support checks and not come dropping around with any awkward questions or annoying instructions.

Freeman calls his plan "supply management." Many of the specifics come from his political mentor, Senator Hubert Humphrey, and from Dr. Willard Cochrane, whom Freeman brought into the Agriculture Department from the University of Minnesota.

The basic Cochrane idea is to have Congress name a fair price for each product and to have a committee of farmers set up a national quota which would supply America's need for the product and yet not permit an oversupply which would cut the price. This national quota then would be divided among the individual farmers. Each farmer could sell in the open market only his quota.

There still would be surpluses, and it is here that Freeman, the administrator and liberal, becomes the right man for the job despite his lack of farming background. Freeman thinks the surplus foods should be used far more as an instrument of foreign aid and also as a means of alleviating hunger in this nation's depressed areas.

This is the happiest of solutions. We have long lived under the paradox that American farmers were producing far too much food while people throughout the world starved. Wouldn't it be the simplest and best solution for the government to buy the excess and give it to those who need it? This would maintain the price for the farmers and feed the hungry.

This is now the administration's aim, but the solution is not as simple as it sounds. It costs considerable money to ship this food overseas and to distribute it upon its arrival. Thus the cost of the farm program increases tremendously. The free distribution of the food in the United States itself might depress the prices of those foods distributed. And there are only certain products which are in surplus. It would be a cruel delusion to think that even the most generous distribution of the surplus would provide an adequate diet for the hungry either here or abroad.

Freeman contends, nevertheless, that the proper way to maintain prices is to take the food from the open market and distribute it to the needy everywhere. The added expense to the farm program would be balanced by the good will the State Department might otherwise have to buy in a different form, he maintains. And if we can't provide a completely balanced diet in this way, at least we can prevent out-and-out starvation.

Freeman figures to be the Cabinet member most embroiled with Congress during the Kennedy administration. This is partly because of the inevitably nasty nature of his job, partly because of the unorthodox nature of his views, and partly because of the stubborn nature of his personality.

Even his best friends have to call him "dedicated" and "deliberate." They say this is what makes him such a good administrator. One ally called him "quite impersonal, even ruthless, in his relations." This, the man told the *Washington Star*, "makes him a good administrator. He doesn't get involved with people."

This attitude got Freeman into more than a few jams while he was serving as governor of Minnesota. He always seemed to start off in the right, or at least from a reasonable position, yet his absolute refusal to compromise made him appear a tyrant in the end.

There was one instance in which the United States Steel Corporation wanted to swap some land it owned for some land the state owned. It seemed like an even deal and the State Land Exchange Commission approved it.

Then Freeman stepped in and demanded that U.S. Steel promise to build an ore reprocessing plant on the swapped land within five years. U.S. Steel said it couldn't make such a promise. Freeman blew his top and not only canceled the deal but fired the entire Land Exchange Commission which had approved the original swap.

His motives were of the best. Minnesota's economy depends heavily on the mining of iron ore in the northern part of the state, and that plant would have been a boon. But his methods were so tough and unyielding that he came off to the voters as a spoiled child.

In 1958 the United Packinghouse Workers struck the Wilson and Company meat-packing plant at Albert Lea. The company tried to keep open, using idle farmers as strike breakers, and Freeman sent in the National Guard to close down the plant at the first sign of violence. A three-judge federal court ordered the plant reopened, saying that Freeman had exceeded his jurisdiction.

Here again he had done nothing wrong in fact; he had only exercised his judgment, even if it was subsequently ruled illegal. But during the ensuing election campaign Freeman insisted that if the same situation arose again, "I would act just as I did at Albert Lea." A governor might become a hero by defying the federal court in Mississippi, but that's not the way they think in Minnesota. Again he seemed to be insisting that his way was the right way and the only right way.

This stubbornness at times tied up the entire state legislature. In Minnesota candidates for the legislature don't run on party lines. But once in office they organize into Liberals and Conservatives. Freeman was, of course, a Liberal. His sworn enemies were the Conservatives.

In 1959 the Conservatives controlled the Senate while the Liberals controlled the House. It should have been obvious that the governor would have to make some sort of peace with the Conservatives to get any legislation through. But Freeman persisted in carrying on a personal vendetta against the Senate Conservatives, and in reprisal they sat on everything the Liberal House proposed. The result was that at the end of its four-month regular session the legislature had accomplished nothing. A two-months special session was necessary, and only then did peace come—on the Senate's terms.

It was this kind of thing which made Minnesota grow tired of Freeman, although by any other standards he was an excellent governor—honest, hard-working, and always looking after the best interests of the people. It was this kind of thing which licked him when he ran for re-election.

Freeman insists that this is the way he must be. "They taught us in the Marines that when you're half-way up a hill in a charge you don't decide maybe you should have attacked on the flank. You just keep going up the hill."

As a campaigner Freeman was handicapped by his obvious distaste for the cheap back-slapping which so many politicians consider essential. He would go through the motions, for he knew he must, but it was always obvious that he would be much happier standing on his record than standing in the cold at a plant gate, waiting to shake the grimy hands of the workers who emerge.

Freeman is the type who wants to do his work until it is done well, and then he wants to go home and enjoy his family. He spends considerable time with his wife and two children, even bicycling with them. When he was governor he insisted on taking two weeks off each year to frolic with his family at a northern Minnesota resort. During that period he cut himself off completely from the capitol and politics.

He is a largish handsome man who dresses conservatively and keeps a carton of milk at his desk to ward off a minor gastric spasm he has had for some time. It appears to be an ulcer, but his doctors have told him repeatedly that it is not.

In large gatherings he proves to be an excellent and forceful speaker. Perhaps his star performance came the night he nominated John Kennedy for President at the 1960 Democratic National Convention in Los Angeles.

Freeman had prepared the speech carefully, and he was so anxious to avoid any slip-ups that he insisted on a run-through to make certain the TelePrompter would move his text at the proper speed for delivery. Then, as the big moment came and Freeman faced the full convention and the huge television audience, the TelePrompter jammed after carrying only the first few lines of the speech. Freeman didn't pause a moment. He continued with fervor, remembering some of his speech and improvising the rest. He was a roaring success.

In private gatherings Freeman comes off as a genial and talkative person but not one of the world's great humorists. He has an inquisitive, probing mind, and his talk most often runs to the serious.

Freeman was born in Minneapolis May 9, 1918. His father operated a men's clothing store which eventually went broke. His grandfather owned a 280-acre farm near Zumbrota, Minnesota, and it is that which serves as Freeman's only link with agriculture. He worked on the farm during his summers as a boy, and he eventually inherited it. Today he operates the farm with a concentration on cattle, hogs, and small grains.

He worked his way through the University of Minnesota as a janitor, a hod carrier, and a parking-lot attendant. He played quarterback on the varsity football team and he made Phi Beta Kappa—but, most important, he met a fellow student from Minnesota by the name of Hubert Humphrey.

They became great pals. Humphrey was the only married man in their set, and Mrs. Humphrey became a sort of den mother to the group of young political zealots who would gather at night for a little coffee and a great deal of conversation. Freeman and Humphrey had decided already that they both would go into politics and, as a matter of fact, they even agreed that one would become governor and the other U.S. Senator. They don't remember now who was supposed to be which.

In August of 1941 Freeman enlisted in the Marine Corps and promptly got a commission as a second lieutenant. He went to Bougainville and there caught a Japanese bullet in the face; he still bears the scar. After the war ended he returned to Minnesota to win his law degree, and upon his graduation he was ready to go to work for his pal, Humphrey. By then Humphrey was mayor of Minneapolis, and Freeman was hired as his assistant.

Before the war Humphrey and Freeman were members of the state's third party, the Farmer-Labor Party; they helped merge it with the Democratic Party. In 1948 Humphrey and Freeman teamed to fight with the old Farmer-Labor group for control of the State Democratic Party. They won, and in the process Humphrey was elected to the Senate while Freeman became the party's top man, first in the capacity of executive secretary and subsequently as state chairman.

But the first two times he ran for office Freeman lost. He was defeated for attorney general in 1950 and for governor in 1952. He felt he had had enough, and when 1954 came he refused to run. Humphrey was up for re-election at the same time, and he pleaded with Freeman to run on the same ticket with him. The discussion lasted until 4 o'clock in the morning, and then Freeman finally capitulated. He won, and in '56 and '58 he was re-elected. By 1960, however, there had been too many feuds, too many fights, and he was defeated.

Although they have been buddies through the years—with a few spats to spice the relationship—Freeman and Humphrey are hardly alike. Humphrey loves the political arena. Freeman just wants to get the job done; he doesn't care for the shenanigans that go with getting elected and keeping the county chairmen happy.

They really share only their liberal political philosophy. Freeman has long been a fighter for equal opportunity for Negroes, even though the sparse population of Negroes in his state means nothing in the way of votes. This is simply his belief, and Orville Freeman will always fight for his beliefs, no matter where he is or what the consequences.

As a friend put it, "This guy has never run from a fight and he never will."

Chapter Twelve

THE SECRETARY OF INTERIOR

THE FIRST THING Stewart Udall did after he was appointed Secretary of the Interior was read Harold Ickes' autobiography. It was encouraging: like Udall, Ickes didn't know anything about the job when he first assumed it, yet he developed into what Udall considers the best Interior Secretary the nation has ever had.

It was not that Udall was unconversant with the basic problems of the department. As a Western Congressman, and furthermore as a member of the House Interior Committee, he could not escape them. But he had only the vaguest idea how these problems were attacked and how this sprawling department was administered.

Udall is no longer vague. He now knows where he is going and it's a destination which has intrigued him all of his adult life.

The Interior Department, charged primarily with the development and conservation of natural resources, operates on such a vast scale that its actions invariably fly over the head of the average voter and also, for that matter, the average Congressman. For this reason the Secretary of Interior has a particularly responsible job. Although in theory he is no different than any other Cabinet officer, in fact he is free from the usual inspection of government watchdogs because the dogs don't understand what they are watching. The result has been such extremes as Ickes, who was a fanatical defender of the public's resources; Albert Fall, whose department produced the notorious Teapot Dome scandal; and Douglas McKay, whose department was open to plunderers as long as they didn't do anything illegal.

Udall is no Ickes, principally because he doesn't have the raspy personality and ranging ego of Ickes, but his policies certainly reflect those of Ickes. Udall is a typical Kennedy liberal, dedicated to the cause but also laden with the political savvy and the willingness to compromise when prudence dictates.

The matter of producing more water for the dry West is a major concern of the Interior Department, and here Udall's attitudes are illustrated best. First of all, he wants that water for the immediate problem of irrigation; after all, he is from Arizona. But Udall also looks beyond the deserts of Arizona to the deserts of Africa.

He says, "If we could beat the Russians to finding a low-cost efficient way of making salt water usable, this could be far more important in some areas of the world than competition on the fringe of space."

This is the kind of thinking Adlai Stevenson seeks when he says we should use the United Nations as an agency for helping potential allies. It is the kind of thinking which could make the U.S. a dominant power not on the basis of military strength but on the basis of technical strength.

Quite obviously, the way to ease the water shortage which plagues vital areas of the world is to convert the inexhaustible supply of sea water into fresh water. This can be done now, but not economically. The conversion method must be cheap or else it is no solution to the problem. The Interior Department until now has been spending $3,000,000 a year in research, a paltry sum in view of the immensity of the problem and the great benefits to be derived from its solution. Udall is stepping up this research in the interests of "future generations of all Americans" as well as those who already live in an area of thirst. As the population grows and more water is used up, the time will come when shortages will plague the entire nation rather than only the desert West.

At the same time that he seeks out the ultimate goal of converting sea water into fresh, Udall intends a continuing program to halt pollution of rivers and streams throughout the nation. Here is a case not of natural shortage but of outright waste. This is hardly a regional problem. All of Congress can be rather intimately affected when the wind blows the stench off the Potomac right in the nation's capital.

Aside from water, Udall has an abiding interest in the woeful plight of the American Indians. As a Congressman he had 100,000 Indians in his home district, and so it was not surprising to hear him say, perhaps a little indelicately, "I suppose that in a way I'm going to be my own Indian Commissioner."

Udall immediately called for a new approach to the Indian. He said, "We need above all to realize that there isn't 'an Indian problem.' But there are tons of specific problems on each Indian reservation. We must solve these one by one. We need more understanding to work with the Indians. What we really want is to help them help themselves.

"The need is not so much for a big new national policy as for more brainpower. We need thought and responsibility at the reservation—from the Indians themselves and from the Indian Bureau people on the spot."

Thus Udall has decentralized Indian affairs somewhat. He has adopted the plan which a group of 12 Indian tribes called for at the start of his administration: "More authority must be placed at the field agency level."

Udall, as a self-styled liberal, naturally leans toward public power in the old controversy of whether to develop the West with public projects such as the TVA or private projects. His contention principally is that private power should certainly operate where it can, but that some power needs are too big for any private company to fill; he feels that the government must step in to provide power in these instances rather than have the area wait amid a power shortage for the years and even decades it would take private power to produce what's needed.

Udall also has launched a new public parks plan, a system to provide more recreation areas for Americans throughout the nation. His major concern here is the seashore. Just as the hotels have gobbled up almost every inch of the Miami Beach waterfront, so the nation's entire seashore is being consumed by private interests. It is the plan of the Kennedy administration—first expressed by Kennedy during the campaign and now inherited by Udall as Interior Department policy—for the government to buy up large strips of seashore and maintain these as free beaches for the general public. It is a massive operation but, Udall says, "We're not afraid of big programs if they're in the national interest." It must be a quick operation, too. "The seashores are going rapidly as it is," Udall says.

While the seashore is the more pressing concern because of the race against private buyers for the open space which still remains, the Udall recreation plan also calls for more national parks inland, too.

A good deal of the Interior Department's plans depend on the national economy. Here Interior prospers when the rest of the nation is in want. The reason is simple politics: Interior can get the money for many additional projects only when a recession is on and the government is going out of its way to spend money in order to make jobs and hypo the economy. It was through the public works projects that Ickes became such a power during Franklin D. Roosevelt's administrations. President Eisenhower ordered something of a public works speed-up during the 1958 recession, but Udall feels it was too little too late to do either the economy or the Interior Department any significant good.

Personally, Udall is what's now known around Washington as "the typical Kennedy type"—young, liberal, bright, but, as one capital observer put it, "controllable and loyal to the team." This Kennedy breed plays to win, and there were times during the election campaign when Udall seemed to go overboard. One liberal who was wavering between convention support for Kennedy and Stevenson got Udall's "absolute promise" that Senator Hubert Humphrey would become majority leader if Kennedy became President. This was a promise which Udall had no hope, let alone chance, of keeping. But he was playing to win and couldn't stop short of the impossible when dangling promises before his prospects.

There is no doubt, however, that Udall is a deep and sincere believer in the liberal causes. He was far more active in Congress as a member of the House Education and Labor Committee than on the Interior Committee, for these were the issues which moved him most. Udall frequently fought for liberal causes which were of no political help to him. He was, for example, a hard fighter in the cause of getting the vote for residents of the District of Columbia. Udall had absolutely nothing to gain here. His home base is in Arizona and even his Washington residence is out of the District in suburban Virginia. But he felt that the cause was right, and so he fought for it as avidly as if he had been battling for something which would benefit his constituents in Arizona.

Udall is a man who likes to study problems before he tackles them. It was typical of him to burrow in that three-volume Ickes autobiography to learn just what an Interior Secretary is and how he is expected to operate. Udall, the avid reader, also was the man who brought poet Robert Frost into the Kennedy inauguration ceremonies.

In a typical Washington circumstance, the elderly Frost was engaged as a consultant to the Library of Congress because somebody thought it would be a nice idea. That was the end of that. In a newspaper interview, Consultant Frost complained nobody ever consulted him about anything. Thousands of people read that newspaper story, but only Udall did something about it.

He telephoned Frost and said he'd love to consult the poet about a number of things. They met at Udall's home and quickly became fast friends. Udall thus suggested to Kennedy that Frost participate in the inauguration and Kennedy readily agreed to the idea.

It was, ironically, through a defeat that Udall first became close to John Kennedy. The issue was the labor reform bill of 1959. Udall was one of a group of five on the House Labor Committee plumping for an "effective but moderate" bill. Kennedy was the leader of companion forces in the Senate. Arrayed against them were powerful lobbies, on one hand seeking no reform bill at all and on the other seeking to use labor reform as an excuse to railroad through Congress a bevy of anti-labor restrictions. The five on the House committee who pushed for a moderate bill—they began calling themselves "the fearless five"—held the balance of power between the two extremes and hence were under special pressure. "We were called all sorts of names," Udall says.

The moderates eventually lost. The tougher Landrum-Griffin bill passed the Congress. But in the strategy meetings

Udall got to know Kennedy quite well. "I liked the way his mind worked, the way he attacked a problem and stuck with it," Udall says. "I decided he was the man we needed."

So at 3 A.M., the night Congress adjourned in 1959, Udall dropped by Kennedy's office in the Capitol and "told him I wanted him to be President." The idea had occurred to Kennedy before, about three years before, but he welcomed the new recruit to the ranks.

Udall became a key man in the campaign. He first proved his mettle by whisking away Arizona's 11 convention votes from the very grip of Lyndon Johnson and awarding them to Kennedy. This was quite a coup, for Johnson's real strength was in the South and Southwest.

Then, when Kennedy won the nomination and selected Johnson as his running mate, Udall showed his persuasive powers again. As the delegates convened in Los Angeles' Sports Arena for the session to nominate a Vice President, there were dark mutterings over Kennedy's choice. One staunch Kennedy backer went on the radio to plead publicly with the Senator to change his mind and dump Johnson. The California and Michigan delegates especially were threatening to revolt against the Kennedy choice and to demand an open ballot for the Vice Presidential nomination. Through all of this turmoil Udall slipped from delegation to delegation cajoling, pleading, promising, reassuring—and when the voting began there was no fight: It was Johnson with almost a benevolent smile from the liberals.

Udall was not the only man responsible for the change. To be sure, he was only one of numerous lieutenants sent out to nip the uprising. But his particular efforts were so effective that, once again, he endeared himself to John Kennedy.

Few of Kennedy's Congressional friends would even consider a Cabinet position after the election. They feared these as dead ends. But Udall could take such a job, for as Interior Secretary he can retain ties with his local electorate. The problems of water supply, power supply, and the like are of constant major concern, and thus the Interior Secretary, who may be a name vaguely recalled in the East, is a regular page-one figure in the West.

When Udall took the Interior portfolio, many considered it a step forward toward either the governorship of Arizona or, more likely, the U.S. Senate. The political purists are intrigued by the prospects of an election pitting undiluted conservative Barry Goldwater against undiluted liberal Stewart Udall. This could happen in Arizona in 1964.

Udall was born January 31, 1920, in St. Johns, Arizona, a small town he seldom left until he completed high school. He stems from two pioneer Mormon families. His father was a self-taught lawyer who eventually became chief justice of the state supreme court. "To him public service was a way of life," Stewart says. So many Udalls are lawyers and judges in Arizona today that court dockets frequently must be changed in order that one Udall lawyer won't be opposing another or that a Udall lawyer won't be trying a case before a Udall judge.

Stewart Udall served during the war as an enlisted gunner on a B-24 and then, in contrast, he devoted two years to work as a missionary for the Mormon Church in New York and Pennsylvania. He attended Eastern Arizona College for a year and then the University of Arizona.

For all the talk of the Kennedy touch-football regime, Udall is actually the star athlete of the Cabinet. He played on Arizona's basketball team which went to the Madison Square Garden invitational tournament in 1946. It met Kentucky, then the Notre Dame of basketball, and that "was the last basketball I ever played," Udall recalls ruefully. It was just as well. Neither Udall nor the Arizona team did anything to diminish Kentucky's reputation.

Udall still looks athletic. He is a stocky and rugged-appearing fellow with close-cropped hair and a skin usually well tanned. Around Washington he generally wears the suits of the young businessman, but he occasionally shows up in ten-gallon hat and Western boots.

Upon his graduation from Arizona in 1948 he went into law practice with his brother in Tucson. In 1954 he ran for Congress for the first time and was elected. He remained in the House until he resigned to take the Cabinet position.

Udall, who had been a Stevenson supporter before he came under the Kennedy spell, already looks to the time when he'll be beating the bushes again for Kennedy in 1964. Since Kennedy appeared weakest in the West in 1960, the proportions of Udall's assignment are obvious.

Meanwhile there is work, much work, to be done in the Interior Department, but Udall can be expected to kill two birds with one stone. He feels that his success with the department will to a large extent determine his success with the Western voters when election time returns.

Chapter Thirteen

THE SECRETARY OF HEALTH,
EDUCATION AND WELFARE

In 1950 Congressman Abraham Ribicoff of Connecticut voted against the plan to establish a Secretary of Health, Education and Welfare. Exactly ten years later, Governor Abraham Ribicoff of Connecticut was asked what job he wanted in the Kennedy administration and he unhesitatingly chose to become Secretary of Health, Education and Welfare.

This classic contradiction doesn't embarrass Abe Ribicoff in the least. It only goes to prove, he says, that "a lot of us can be wrong at any given time." Ribicoff is accommodating that way. He often speaks of "the integrity of compromise."

It is his contention that when the "clamor and shouting" die down, the opposing groups on any issue in American politics are not nearly so far apart as they think. He feels this is especially true in the areas which concern him now, principally federal aid to education and old-age medical insurance.

When Ribicoff went into office he set as his special goal a solution of the problem of health costs. He said, "It would be tragic for us to admit, in the richest nation in the world, that the benefits of health care are too expensive for our people." He is concerned not only with doctor bills and hospital bills but also with the cost and inaccessibility of medical education. He wants more medical schools and he wants the government to help finance needy students through these schools. He wants to reverse the trend whereby only children of the rich can aspire to become doctors.

Ribicoff's credentials for his job are in his record as governor of Connecticut. He was a doer. When he speaks of federal aid to education, it is from the experience of a man who almost tripled state aid to education during his two terms in office. When he speaks of aids to mental health, he can point to a 100-per-cent increase in such aid while he was in the State House at Hartford. When he speaks of compassion for the aged, his words are bolstered by accomplishments: Connecticut has one of the nation's most comprehensive medical-care programs for the aged, it has a special commission to handle other problems of the aged, and it has a special low-cost housing program for the aged.

Despite his ironic opposition to its creation in 1950, the Health, Education and Welfare Department actually embraces all of the interests which Ribicoff has in government. He set out his program when he was first nominated for governor in 1954:

> We need moral vision to undertake the responsibilities and financial burdens of educating our children. . . .
>
> We need moral vision to see the alcoholic not as a criminal, but as a sick human being who needs love and care and rehabilitation.
>
> We need moral vision to see our jails and our correctional institutions not as dust-bins for the sweepings of society, but as rehabilitation centers.
>
> We need moral vision to see our older people not as derelicts of life, but as the image of our future selves.

Ribicoff defied many an entrenched system while instituting reforms in Connecticut. He abolished the inefficient and often corrupt city and town courts and replaced them with the first state circuit court system in the nation. He did this despite the political power of the unfrocked judges and despite the fact that Abraham Ribicoff himself had once served as a police court judge under the old system.

He launched one of the nation's most effective highway safety campaigns. His method was simple: he put real teeth into enforcement by taking up the licenses of all drivers convicted of speeding. His fellow Democratic politicians blanched at the original suggestion, for Connecticut was a state of thousands of speedsters who used the parkways into and out of New York as raceways; every lost license was a lost vote, the politicians warned. But Ribicoff felt he was taking the calculated risk that his program would produce slower driving rather than mass license suspensions. He turned out to be correct. The percentage of voters who lost licenses was small and Ribicoff had no need to worry about their votes.

"I'm a wholesaler of votes, not a retailer," he said. He was also a saver of lives. The Connecticut highway death toll went down steadily after the Ribicoff safety program went into effect.

The governor showed great ability to follow through a problem until it was solved. He had been in office only a few months when a hurricane and resultant floods lashed the state. Ribicoff rallied recovery forces and announced that the worst disaster in Connecticut's history would be turned into an advantage. It would be the excuse to build "a better state."

Any governor would have mouthed such words under the circumstances, but Ribicoff meant them. He called the legislature into a special emergency session and pushed through a plan for modernization of the stricken towns and for reconstruction and expansion of the washed-out highways and bridges. Connecticut rebuilt facilities which otherwise would have deteriorated without interference for years.

Ribicoff pressed so hard for medical and welfare progress that the state soon was spending nearly 75 per cent of its total budget for that purpose. But he was not nearly so adept at making money as he was at spending it. He sold the people on these benefits partly because he promised to produce them without raising taxes. He succeeded, but he "got out of the state just in time," one critic says. His successor was faced with the need of a $130,000,000 tax increase to pay the bills that Ribicoff's programs were running up.

Ribicoff is a tough man to work for. He is a perfectionist who drives himself and his subordinates ruthlessly. He has no patience with failure. When he was governor, various heads of the state agencies received blistering telephone calls on the subject of their misdeeds, and on at least two of these occasions the governor had newspapermen in his office while he was tongue-lashing a department head.

Ribicoff has always had great success with the press. This is partly because he works at it and partly because he has the professional's knack of public relations. In Connecticut's Fairfield County, traditional home of many of New York's top public relations and advertising men, one of them once cracked, "Abe Ribicoff is a public relations man who happens to be governor." For the first few years of his administration as governor, Ribicoff didn't have a press secretary because he felt he could do the job best himself. He was right. And he made certain that the press was always on hand to cover his activities. If the reporters' newspapers wouldn't finance their trips with the governor across the state and to national governors' conferences, Ribicoff would pay the travel expenses himself.

He not only talked to reporters but he listened to them. He learned a great deal about how to handle news, when to announce it, and how to spoon-feed it over a long period of time.

Ribicoff was always prepared to use the press to further his programs as governor, and when he decided to move from Hartford into a position of national prominence, he simply changed presses. Suddenly the Connecticut reporters who had traveled with him and covered his office daily found the news stories going to the big national publications and big out-of-state newspapers. The governor had simply promoted himself.

At the same time that Ribicoff was seducing the masses through the press, he developed a special technique of buttering up the state's bigshots of any political stripe. He would frequently telephone top executives, some of whom he had never met, to ask their advice on state programs. No man is such a bigshot that he isn't flattered when the governor calls to ask *his* advice. Those telephone calls got Ribicoff support from the most unlikely sources.

This was part of Ribicoff's smokescreen of "unpartisanship" in the governor's office. Actually, he gave out virtually all of the paid patronage jobs to Democrats and then decorated his administration by placing Republicans on fancy-titled commissions which paid nothing and carried little or no authority.

But when Ribicoff faced a particularly delicate political problem he would make this "nonpartisanship" work for him. He would find a Republican who agreed with him on the issue in question, appoint that man to a study commission, and subsequently announce "recommendations from a commission headed by Mr. Blank, a leading Republican."

Once he was established as governor, Ribicoff rationed his public appearances. He guarded against "overexposure" and he concentrated as much as he could on the administrative work in the office rather than the handshaking work in the field.

He is an excellent public speaker. One reason for this is his insistence on talking not from a prepared text but off the cuff. "I like to size up the audience and see how they react," he says. "Then I can adjust my remarks accordingly."

Some of these adjustments have been little short of fantastic. Once when he was addressing a predominantly Republican audience he devoted 45 minutes to comparing himself to Abraham Lincoln. Says one man who was present, "I'll be damned if those people didn't leave the hall thinking Ribicoff was Abe Lincoln."

Connecticut politicians say it was a single speech which overcame Ribicoff's greatest handicap when he first began his campaign for the governorship. Ribicoff is a Jew and no Jew had ever been elected governor of the state. Gradually anti-Semitism seeped into the campaign, but Ribicoff halted it with one moving address on "the American dream." His success in defeating the anti-Semitism issue was studied carefully by Kennedy people when they were confronted with the anti-Catholicism of the 1960 national campaign.

Ribicoff has spent much time proving himself to be a moderate. It is partly for this reputation that Kennedy chose him for the delicate Health, Education and Welfare position in the Cabinet. But this position of the moderate has left Ribicoff open to criticism from both the left and the right.

A Connecticut liberal says Ribicoff "is the only guy in the world who has built a political career out of praise for traffic safety, religious holidays, patriotism and Flag Day." A Connecticut conservative says Ribicoff "has switched sides on so many issues that I can't list them. He is nothing but an opportunist."

This may well be, but there is no doubt that Ribicoff has been successful at his saunter down the middle of the road. When he first ran for governor of Connecticut, he won by a scant 3,300 votes. Four years later he was re-elected by a record-smashing margin of 346,000 votes, and few denied that he could have won a third term with ease had he not elected to go to Washington instead.

Ribicoff was among the very first supporters of Kennedy for President. He and John Bailey, now the Democratic National Chairman, first urged the Senator for President in 1956. They got nowhere then, but they advised him often during the ensuing four years, which led to the nomination at the 1960 convention.

Furthermore, when the election came, Ribicoff and Bailey delivered. That, not nominating speeches or campaign train rides, is the real test of a politician's support. Connecticut was the first state to report full returns on election night, and these gave Kennedy a 92,000 majority in the state. At his headquarters in Hyannis Port, Massachusetts, Kennedy whooped with joy at the news, and from that moment on there was no doubt that Ribicoff would get what he wanted from the new administration. He was the first man summoned to Kennedy's Palm Beach home after the election, and his was the first Cabinet appointment announced.

Ribicoff is a man who takes care of himself physically as well as politically. "I'm no superman," he says, and is careful to keep his office hours and his recreation hours well apart. He is a punctual man and in this instance hardly fits in with the Kennedy regime, which generally runs an hour late on everything.

Ribicoff will call a meeting for 9 o'clock and be there at 9. When the department head with whom he is to confer opens the meeting with some small talk, Ribicoff is apt to interrupt with "let's get down to business."

He is a serious-minded man. He doesn't tell jokes and frequently doesn't get the point when someone else tells him one. His wife, on the other hand, is a motherly type who exudes warmth to everyone she meets. While Abe Ribicoff would rush reporters through in a press conference at his home, Ruth Ribicoff would block the newspapermen at the door as they were about to hasten back to their offices with the story. "Stay and have some tea," she'd say. "Take time to relax."

Her husband is a golfer who plays in the 80's. He enjoys massages and lots of sleep on an early-to-bed schedule. He walks quite a bit in the manner of Harry Truman, at a fast clip through all sorts of neighborhoods, some he has tramped regularly and some he is exploring for the first time. He likes the theater and good music and he'll take an occasional drink but never a cigarette or cigar.

Ribicoff was born April 9, 1910, in a cold-water flat at New Britain, Connecticut. His father was a Russian immigrant with scant funds, and so young Abe sold newspapers and delivered groceries to bolster the family income. He got as far as college, but after a year he had to quit and go to work. His company sent him to Chicago as a salesman, but at night he continued his studies until he graduated from the University of Chicago Law School.

He returned to Hartford to practice law and quickly immersed himself in ward politics. He probably has more bottom-level knowledge of politics than anyone in the top echelon of the Kennedy administration. He served two terms in the state legislature and two as a police court judge before John Bailey wangled his big break.

Bailey first convinced Ribicoff he ought to run for Congress in Hartford's First District. Then Bailey had to talk the Democratic bosses into accepting Ribicoff as the nominee.

The year was 1948. Everyone anticipated a sweeping Thomas Dewey victory over Truman, and it was assumed that Dewey would carry a Republican Congress into Washington with him. Ribicoff campaigned on the housing issue—this was at the peak of the postwar shortage—and then he sat back to await the dismal result.

Truman won, and Ribicoff won, too. Some of Ribicoff's cronies rushed to his campaign headquarters to join the victory party, but they found nothing to eat and nothing to drink. No one had thought to order any refreshments for a victory party. No one had anticipated a victory.

Ribicoff served in the House from 1948 to 1952, and then a Republican sweep did engulf him. When Eisenhower was elected President, Republican Prescott Bush swept into Ribicoff's House seat. He sat out the next two years in his law office and then ran for governor in 1954.

Ribicoff is especially proud of his political success in view of the handicaps he had to overcome because of his religion. He is deeply religious and frequently addresses both synagogues and Congregational churches.

Ribicoff's influence in Washington goes beyond his own job in the Cabinet. He has been an advisor to Kennedy for a long time, and his advice has never gone wrong. He is consulted on many issues, particularly political, that don't necessarily fall in the realm of his department. One reason he seems to know all the answers is that he studies every problem in detail. He can often discuss a bill with more knowledge of its small print than the Congressman who introduced it.

But above all Ribicoff always lets it be known that he is accommodating and willing to listen to compromise. When he was a Congressman himself, he introduced a bill calling for price supports for shade tobacco, a Connecticut product. He was presenting this bill because his constituents asked him to, he said on the floor of the House, but that didn't mean he was for it; as a matter of fact, Ribicoff said, he intended to vote against his own bill.

It was a clever stunt. The shade tobacco growers were not of much voting consequence anyway, and Ribicoff meanwhile had advertised his reputation for fairness and integrity.

This is the kind of thinking Kennedy wanted in the Department of Health, Education and Welfare. This is the kind of thinking Kennedy feels is necessary to push the administration's welfare program through a cautious and moderate Congress.

Ribicoff accepts the task with eagerness, and he already envisions his reward. He wants to conclude his career on the Supreme Court. With that prize in mind, he is one of the busiest beavers in the administration.

Chapter Fourteen

THE POSTMASTER GENERAL

POSTMASTER GENERAL J. Edward Day is the type of man who likes to puncture myths. He went to Washington billed as "a former law partner of Adlai Stevenson"; actually, Day says, he was once a clerk in the firm which listed Stevenson as one of many partners. He was advertised as a wartime Navy hero; actually, he says, he saw very little "real action." He was celebrated as the new white hope of the Post Office Department because he was a businessman who could bring efficiency to that debt-ridden department; actually, Day says, the Post Office Department can't be run like an ordinary business and besides "not all private businesses are businesslike."

The position of Postmaster General has, in the past, been usually reserved for unabashed political pay-off by both Republican and Democratic administrations. Day's appointment certainly was not without its politics, for he was the nominee of California's Governor Pat Brown, to whom Kennedy was beholden. However, Kennedy made the selection in the genuine hope that Day's combination of government and business experience might add some efficiency and subtract some red ink from the antiquated department. Kennedy remarked wryly on the afternoon he appointed Day that it had taken a letter eight days to get from Washington to Boston.

Day's efforts to shore up the Post Office Department are

somewhat stymied by a conflict of forces constantly at work. The department spends more than it makes, yet there is constant resistance by Congress to any plan to raise revenue by increasing postal rates and constant pressure from the powerful post office employees' lobby to further increase expenses by pay hikes.

The Post Office Department is supposed to lose money. Everyone agrees on that. It carries the mail as a service to the citizens just as the Fire Department extinguishes fires free of charge as a service to the citizenry. But how much money should it lose? There is no agreement here. Its delivery of publications for extremely low rates and its backbreaking load of through-the-mails advertising have been questioned; are these, too, services to the public or are they subsidizations of private business?

Furthermore, delivery of the mail is just one function of the Post Office Department. In addition to transporting letters and packages through every means available (including helicopter, horseback, and dogsled), the Post Office operates a banking service (through its postal savings and money order systems), it sells hunting stamps, it issues flags for veterans' funerals, and, for some incomprehensible reason, it is in charge of registering aliens.

Day does not delude himself into thinking he can mold all of this into a sharply efficient and profitable operation, but he did launch his administration with the conviction that he can improve things somewhat. It's all a matter of standing firm. "Management must manage," he said. "We will listen to reason and, where necessary, will have the courage to say 'no' frankly and without rancor."

He launched an austerity campaign, a move toward "elimination of waste and frills." He said, "We seek ways to eliminate needless expense. Already we see that we can cut down on department spending for motion pictures, for publicity, and for outside management consultant firms."

Mail delivery is slow largely because Post Office employees do many things by hand which could be done faster and better by machines. For several administrations Postmasters General have been toying with the idea of automation; they have so hungered for it, in fact, that at times they would invest in the wildest kind of machine in hope that *it just might* prove workable. Day thinks a great deal of money has been wasted this way. He said:

> Our main interest in automation and mechanical equipment will be to improve working conditions for better service. I do not consider that I was appointed Postmaster General merely to preside over an aggregation of machines. Of course we will experiment with new equipment. But we do not plan to finance all the research and experimentation.
>
> We will expect suppliers to present us, at least part of the time, with tried and proven equipment and methods, and not merely with suggested experiments for us to subsidize. We are not interested in gadgets and gimmicks for their own sake. With our programs for improved equipment and facilities, as with our other programs, our emphasis will be upon proven results and not on promotion and promises.

One thing Day seeks in the Post Office Department is the friendship of the public. In his first talk to the headquarters staff at Washington he said, "It will do us good to sparkle a bit—even, at times, to show that we have a sense of humor."

The Postmaster General is, in effect, the nation's Number One censor in that he rules on what matter cannot be sent through the mails because it is obscene. Since the only practical way to ship books is through the mail, this is a great power.

Arthur Summerfield, the Eisenhower Postmaster General, became rabid on the subject. He spent many hours justifying his decisions. He even kept a large collection of pornographic material in his office to show visitors just how vile the purveyors can get. This was dubbed "the museum" by other people in the department, and there were dark suspicions that some of Summerfield's visitors professed an interest in the anti-obscenity campaign just so they could get a peek at the horrible examples. Day has no intention of letting down the bars on obscene material, but he did banish the "museum" material back into the department files and indicated that he'd devote less time to the drive than Summerfield did.

Day insists he has never read *Lady Chatterly's Lover* and consequently could not discuss the most celebrated case in which Summerfield was embroiled. But Day himself is a bona fide author. While he was in the Navy on Atlantic convoy duty during World War II he wrote a novel entitled *Bartholf Street*, the story of a young doctor who, in the author's words, "was something of a heel." The book sold less than 1,000 copies, but undismayed Day has ambitions to write another when he finds the time.

The slim, white-haired Postmaster General is able to accomplish tremendous loads of work. "He is the best-organized guy I know," said one friend. He works fast, never looks back on yesterday's successes or failures, and insists upon bypassing the little problems so that he can concentrate on the big ones. "The man who worries is probably in the wrong work," he says. "I never feel pressured or the need to escape. If I ever found myself in a mountain cabin I'd hitchhike right back to the city."

Adlai Stevenson, for whom Day worked in the Illinois state government and in Presidential election campaigns, described him as "a fellow with great wit, humor and geniality, with a sharp, incisive mind and an infinite capacity for work."

The practice of showing no concern for a problem until it is big enough to demand attention has always been a Day trait. An old schoolmate recalls that Day was always poor in mathematics until the school put up a math prize. "Then he got his fine mind to work and won it. He was just bored until there was a challenge."

Day first attracted attention as Insurance Commissioner in his native Illinois. He had been serving Stevenson, who was governor, as a legal and legislative assistant when he chanced to have dinner one night with Stevenson and Edward Rust, president of the State Farm Insurance Company. Stevenson mentioned to Rust that he was looking for a new Insurance Commissioner to replace the one who had just resigned. Rust said, "I wouldn't look for anyone experienced. I'd try to find a hard-hitting young lawyer."

Day was driving Stevenson home from the dinner when he said, "I heard what Rust said about the Insurance Commissioner. That sounds like me."

Stevenson agreed, and Day was given the job. He quickly learned what a lion the Insurance Commissioner is. Company executives came calling in droves. During the Christmas season of 1950, Day was startled to see that gifts poured into his office—whisky, luggage, cigarette lighters, ashtrays, cheese, fruit. He was embarrassed but didn't know quite what to do. He remarked that he was at least glad there was no mink coat amidst the loot.

The next Christmas he headed off the influx. In advance he wrote to the insurance companies, asking them to omit him from their holiday list. He was doubly grateful for this foresight when he found himself exposing an insurance racket of great proportions. He might have been beholden to the very companies he prosecuted had he not stemmed the tide of largesse.

As it was Day got into hot water over the matter of a $2,000 "gift."

After disclosure of the "Nixon fund" caused such a furor in the 1952 election campaign, it came to light that there was something of a "Stevenson fund," too, while he was governor of Illinois. There had been $18,000 left over from the campaign contributions when Stevenson was elected governor, and he distributed this among eight officials in his administration to help make up, he said, what they had lost by leaving private business for government service.

Day got $2,000 of this $18,000. He said he took it as a gift, did not consider it extra salary, and did not declare it on his income-tax return. The furor over this fund and the Nixon fund died with the conclusion of the political campaign.

Upon his graduation from Harvard Law School, Day had joined the firm of Sidley, Austin, Burgess and Harper, and he subsequently married the boss' daughter, Mary Louise Burgess, daughter of Kenneth F. Burgess. When Day's term as Insurance Commissioner expired, his father-in-law urged him to return to the family firm. Day refused.

A friend recalls, "He and his father-in-law went 'round and 'round. Burgess, a convincing lawyer himself, brought up the fact that in the firm Day's future was assured. But Burgess lost every argument. Day told his father-in-law he wanted to strike out for himself and make it on his own. He wouldn't consider it any other way."

He acquired an excellent reputation among the insurance

companies, and the way he spurned the traditional Christmas loot no doubt helped. Prudential was especially interested in Day's services because of his political know-how. The company was planning to invest policy holders' funds in a new manner and wanted someone to explain the change to state insurance commissions. Day was hired to do the job. He was now working the other side of the street from whence he came, but he worked it well.

By 1956 he had been promoted to associate general counsel, and two years later he was made a vice president in charge of the Western States operation. That took Day to Los Angeles. He quickly dug in politically as well as in a business way. He became an active worker in civic projects and one of the leading boosters of Governor Brown. He was a Stevenson delegate to the 1960 convention, but on meeting a friend at the Los Angeles airport a few days before the balloting, he indicated no doubt over who would win the nomination. "Jack Kennedy's a cinch," he said.

Day was born December 11, 1914, as the second of two sons of a country doctor in Jacksonville, Illinois. The family moved to Springfield in 1917, and the day Day was appointed Postmaster General his father, at 91, still lived in the same big white frame house which had served the family for more than 40 years.

Day went to public schools in Springfield and then to the University of Chicago. Although he had come from a family of doctors, it was obvious from his high school debating days that James Edward (he never used the James because "there were too many Jims in the family already") would become a lawyer.

It also became obvious that he would become something of a businessman. He was at the University of Chicago during the 1933 World's Fair. It suddenly struck him that, with so many visitors in town, it was a shame to let the fraternity house sit empty all summer. It could be making money for someone—someone like J. Edward Day. He teamed up with a friend and converted the house into a hostel for Fair visitors. "I made 1,500 beds that summer," he recalls. "I also made a little money."

He graduated from Chicago in 1935 and went to Harvard Law School. He became an editor of the *Harvard Law Review* and one summer he worked in the law office of Brown, Hay and Stephens, a Springfield firm which traces its lineage directly back to Abraham Lincoln's law office.

Day has always dabbled in politics, and it has always been Democratic politics. "I'm a Republican myself," his father snorted with good humor, "but Edward has never been anything except a natural-born Democrat." Day joined the law firm of a southern Illinois Democratic leader upon his graduation from Harvard, but after a few months he went to work for the Burgess office in Chicago.

The Day family of the present consists of three teenagers, two girls and a boy, who are joined together by an insatiable appetite for travel. "We pile into the car and go off somewhere almost every week end," Day says.

He has always been something of an Adlai Stevenson protégé. During the war he was brought to Washington by Stevenson, who then was serving as a special assistant to Secretary of the Navy Frank Knox. Day became a special assistant in the Bureau of Aeronautics, where he worked in a section headed by Arthur Radford, at the time a captain but subsequently chairman of the Joint Chiefs of Staff.

Day had been rebuffed in his bid for active duty because of color blindness, but after a year in Washington he got clearance for sea duty and went aboard a sub-chaser as executive officer. He was on his way to the Pacific for a second tour of duty when the Japanese surrendered.

Day's top assistant in the Post Office Department is a man of considerable experience in the field. H. William Brawley was appointed Deputy Postmaster General by Kennedy after 11 years as staff director and chief clerk of the Senate Committee on Post Office and Civil Service. Before that, he had served as a government cost accountant, an investigator for the Federal Trade Commission, and an administrator for the Small Business Administration. In short, he is a man who knows his way around Washington.

A native of Lockhart, South Carolina, Brawley handled every piece of legislation involving government employees for some five years. Through his work with the Senate Post Office Committee he became known as one of the best-informed men in Washington on the Post Office Department's operations.

The general understanding is that Brawley operates the Post Office Department on a technical basis while Day is the policy maker and the front man to meet Congress and to deal with the White House. Together, they are struggling to see that the mail does go through with reasonable speed at reasonable cost under the most unreasonable handicaps.

Chapter Fifteen

THE REGULATORY AGENCIES

UNDER THE TENT of the big government there are little governments, and within their limited sphere these little governments are far more powerful than the big government would dare to be. The federal regulatory agencies are Supreme Court, Congress, and President to the industries they supervise.

For several years before the Kennedy administration, Congress and outside critics had been firing shotgun blasts at these agencies. Kennedy replaced the shotguns with one big cannon, wielded by James L. Landis, but the agencies still have not fallen or retreated.

The principal agencies involved are the Interstate Commerce Commission, which regulates all transportation except air; the Civil Aeronautics Board, which regulates the airlines' rates and routes; the Federal Aviation Authority, which regulates the planes, pilots, and safety systems; the Securities and Exchange Commission, which regulates stocks, bonds, and their brokers; the Federal Trade Commission, which regulates advertising and business practices; the Federal Communications Commission, which regulates radio and television stations; and the Federal Power Commission, which regulates power and pipe lines and rates.

Landis prepared a pre-inauguration report for Kennedy branding these agencies slow-moving, inefficient, and at times downright dishonest. Kennedy promptly placed Landis on the White House staff to straighten things out—but it hasn't been that easy. There is within each organization the corrosion of years, and furthermore the commissioners at the different agencies each have varying tenures of office which prevent any wholesale reorganization. The most Kennedy could place on any commission at inauguration time was two men; in most cases there was only one vacancy he could fill. Complete replacement of the holdovers takes four to eight years.

Landis blasted the agencies for their outmoded and laborious procedures, but he found far more fault with the quality of men who received commission appointments and the way they permitted their agencies to be governed by the very industries they were supposed to be governing. Too often, these commissioners go into their jobs already beholden to the industry they must regulate; just as often they leave their federal jobs to take fat positions with the regulated industry. Jerome Kuykendall, a lawyer for firms involved in power rate cases, became chairman of the Federal Power Commission in the Eisenhower administration. Edward Howrey, a lawyer for firms with cases before the Federal Trade Commission, became chairman of the FTC. Albert M. Cole, a former Congressman who was an announced foe of public housing, became administrator of the federal housing agency.

The usual complaint is that the government cannot get top-flight or disinterested men because it doesn't pay well enough. Landis scoffs at this. "The salaries run around $20,000 a year," he says. "That is a reasonable salary. The universities get the best caliber at that price. Why can't government do the same thing?"

The Kennedy government has instituted one major reform in the appointment of regulatory agency commissioners: where once the man sought the job, now the job seeks the man; where once the commissionership went to the opportunist or industry front-man who made the most influential application, now the White House seeks, on its own initiative, first-rank men of integrity.

But putting honest and bright men on the commissions is not the only solution to the problem of the regulatory agencies. Nor is the elimination of red tape and understaffing the panacea. There remains the difficult problem of getting both sides of every story to each commission.

Landis said, "You sit at a desk and handle these cases and it's always the industry that comes in to see you. The public is never there, and when the poor public is there, the public is not very intelligent in its comments, and you tend to get a sort of industry viewpoint unless you're very careful. By that I don't mean to criticize the integrity of any individual, but it just happens that way. It's like being subjected to machine-gun fire all the time from one source."

Landis' answer to this is a public counsel, appointed and paid by the government but representing the general public in any hearings before the regulatory agencies. It takes an expert to deal with them since the subjects involved are usually so technical. Landis points out that even Washington law firms which specialize in regulatory agency cases keep their field narrowed to only certain agencies; they know nothing about the procedures and regulations of the boards with which they do not deal. Obviously, if a Washington law firm finds unfamiliar agencies too technical to deal with, poor John Q. Public has no chance of representation unless someone hires an expert to plead his cause.

It would be bad enough if these regulatory agencies, by kowtowing to industry, ignored the general public's interests in the process of making these industries profitable. But, as it turns out, the industries frequently are in miserable financial plight, even under the aegis of beneficent regulation. Despite the ICC's kindness, the railroads are in the worst shape in their history. Despite the CAB's benevolence, most airlines operate in the red.

This is because the agencies often operate not in the best interests of the industry as a whole but only in the best interests of a few big operators with an inside track. Lawyers who would never dare to ask favors from a judge outside the courtroom have had no qualms about asking regulatory agency commissioners to conspire against a competitor.

The law forbids a commissioner from having financial interest in the industry he regulates and it forbids him to accept a bribe. But it does not prevent an opportunist from feathering his nest by issuing a favorable ruling for a company one year and then going to work for that company at a fat salary the next.

There have been times when Congress and even the White House have lobbied as hard as any Washington lawyer for one firm or one industry. This interference from Capitol Hill and Pennsylvania Avenue has always been a major hazard of the regulatory agency business.

Landis found, however, that the lack of professional integrity and resistance to pressure was only one problem of the agencies. There was also the matter of inefficiency. He said the Interstate Commerce Commission decisions are issued flatly with no adequate explanation of law and consequently even the people in the industry often don't understand how the decision was reached. He said the Civil Aeronautics Board "pursues no pattern or plan" in assigning routes and indulges in "inordinate delay" in awarding them. He said the Federal Power Commission is so slow-moving that "thousands of rate cases dealing with independent gas production clutter its docket."

As a move toward efficiency, President Kennedy selected the executive of a sales management firm, John W. Bush, to the first vacancy on the Interstate Commerce Commission. Bush had considerable experience in government in Ohio. He was the state's Director of Commerce at the time of his appointment. At the same time, Landis called for a permanent chairman of the ICC. For years the 11 commissioners took turns serving a year as chairman. Things reached the point, Landis said, where not even the men in the railroad and trucking industry knew who was chairman at any given time.

The chairman of the Federal Communications Commission is Newton N. Minow, a 34-year-old Chicago attorney with practically no previous experience in the broadcasting industry. Under the prod of the publicity which followed the quiz-show scandals, the FCC had taken a turn toward tougher regulation before the Kennedy administration took over. It instituted a program to review the performance of stations before renewing their licenses, for example. Minow said the federal agencies, his own and others, "have got to move faster." But, at the same time, he said that he would prefer to see the broadcast industry regulate itself rather than have the FCC always on its neck enforcing a raft of specific directives.

The Federal Trade Commission is something of a companion organization to the FCC in that it is charged with the elimination of false and unethical advertising, one of TV's major problems. Paul Rand Dixon was selected by Kennedy as the FTC chairman. Dixon, as general counsel to Senator Kefauver's Senate Antimonopoly Subcommittee, had directed investigations of price-fixing in the milk, steel, and automobile industries.

The two most heated enemies in Washington bureaucracy are the Civil Aeronautics Board and the Federal Aviation

Authority. The CAB assigns routes and rates to the airlines, and it investigates accidents; the FAA licenses the pilots, inspects the planes, directs the airport towers, and operates the traffic system. The need for co-operation between these two agencies is obvious, yet the only thing they seem to be able to exchange is venom.

The difficulty, of course, is jealousy. Both agencies operate within the same industry, and thus it is inevitable that they frequently step upon one another's toes. The Kennedy administration planned a study to determine if these two might not be combined.

The head of the FAA is Najeeb Halaby, who served as chief aide to Elwood (Pete) Quesada, the agency's commissioner during the Eisenhower administration. Halaby is a veteran pilot. He flew for the Navy and also served as a test pilot at Lockheed. Halaby has a flair for the dramatic. Amid controversy over whether the Lockheed Electra was safe for full-speed commercial flying, Halaby announced he would settle the problem for himself in a very simple manner: "I'll fly the plane myself up to and beyond the conditions the public will fly in it." He did, and certified the plane as safe.

The chairman of the Securities and Exchange Commission, which was organized in the New Deal days to regulate stock trading so that there would be no repeat of the crash of '29, is William Lucius Clay, who is both a lawyer and holder of a master's degree in business administration. He served on the SEC during the Roosevelt administration, and he also served two years in the Justice Department's tax division.

In addition to the Big Seven agencies specifically charged with the regulation of certain industries, there are many vital independent and quasi-independent agencies in Washington. These have functions ranging from supervision of the federal housing program down here on earth to direction of the space programs way out there.

One of the most vital of these agencies is the Atomic Energy Commission. Its work involves everything from war to peace, from the atomic bombs and submarines to the technicalities of atomic disarmament and the development of atomic power for industrial use.

Its chairman reflects the agency's wide range of concern. Dr. Glenn T. Seaborg helped develop the atomic bomb; as a matter of fact, he and Dr. Edwin McMillan jointly won a Nobel Prize for the work they did. Yet one of his main interests as AEC chairman is finding a way to outlaw the bomb.

As far back as 1956 he wrote, "I am not sure that nuclear disarmament with adequate safeguards against treachery can be achieved, but it is vital that we maintain a continuing evaluation of every possible approach. The appalling waste of the nuclear arms race and its threat of potential utter disaster are two of the central problems that face us in the next decade."

Seaborg had served the AEC as an advisor during the Truman administration, and he was brought back to Washington by Kennedy from the University of California, where he was associate director of the Lawrence Radiation Laboratory.

The AEC has something of a counterpart in the National Aeronautical and Space Administration. This is a baby brother to the AEC and is one of the hottest spots in Washington. The agency is charged with the development of peacetime space projects, as opposed to the Army, Navy, and Air Force military experiments.

But inevitably the NASA work and the military work is

intertwined. There has been frequent pressure to combine all of the efforts into one organization. The aircraft and rocket manufacturers especially yearn for such a combination, since it would give them a central authority with which to deal rather than having to scurry about forever among the different services.

Because the job is such a ticklish one, no fewer than eight persons refused President Kennedy's appeal that they take over NASA. Eventually, however, Kennedy offered the position to James Webb, former Budget Director in the Truman administration and more recently assistant to the president of the Kerr-McGee Oil Industries of Tulsa, Oklahoma. Webb has had considerable experience in the aircraft industry and received the particular endorsement of Jerome B. Wiesner, the White House's chief scientific advisor. Webb nevertheless brought no scientific background to the agency. His experience is all administrative.

On the other hand, the man selected to head the U.S. Information Agency is not much on administration and says so. "Budgets, in-baskets, out-baskets are not for me," quips famed broadcaster Edward R. Murrow.

The information agency has always been a problem and even something of an embarrassment to this country. Its mission obviously is propaganda, and, badly as it is needed, propaganda has always been something of a dirty word to most Americans. In addition to our historic antipathy to the very idea, there is the special suspicion which Congressmen have for any agency which an administration might use to glorify itself.

The USIA, therefore, has always suffered from lack of brains and lack of cash. Murrow may supply the brains, but he doesn't have the cash, even though he gave up a $200,000-a-year income at the Columbia Broadcasting System to take the $21,000 a year at USIA. American propaganda is self-defeating in a way because it is based on honest reporting rather than contrived persuasions. The USIA delivers the bad news as well as the good. Murrow told a Congressional Committee this is the only way USIA can function honestly.

As Murrow reaches into men's minds overseas, Mortimer Caplin reaches into everyone's pocketbook here. As Commissioner of Internal Revenue, he is the administrator of the income tax. He is specifically charged by the Kennedy administration with making tax reforms work.

Caplin, a University of Virginia Law School professor before his appointment, cannot on his own change the tax laws. But he does have complete authority over how the existing laws are administered. He has increased the audits in the department so that now more wage-earners are called to justify their returns, and he has cracked down on the business expense-account deductions. Before he was appointed to the IRS, Caplin had served Kennedy on a study group recommending tax reforms. Many of the subsequent administration tax law change proposals were his suggestions.

Taken together, they all boiled down to one objective: Eliminate the loopholes. IRS agents now take a much tougher view about charitable donations and the like as a result of Caplin's spurs. They also are making a special search for unreported income, such as that which comes from stock and bond dividends.

In seeking talent for second- and third-line jobs in the administration, Kennedy turned not only to the colleges but also to the offices of Congressmen. Numbers of administrative assistants were snatched from Senators and Representatives and placed in the executive branch, where their vast experience in government could be put to work for the Kennedy team.

One of these was Frank McCulloch, who had been administrative assistant to Senator Paul Douglas of Illinois before his appointment as chairman of the National Labor Relations Board. McCulloch had a long history in labor before he went to work for Douglas. During the automobile industry's sit-down strikes of the 1930's, he was industrial relations secretary for the Congregational Church's Council of Social Action in Flint, Michigan. He did considerable work building up an atmosphere for settlement of the strikes.

The touchiest appointment of the Kennedy administration was that of Robert Weaver, a Negro, as Housing and Home Finance Administrator. In the first place, Weaver's appointment came on the heels of the deal to have Representative Dawson, the Negro Congressman from Illinois, turn down the position of Postmaster General so that it could be given to Day; there was an immediate outcry from Negro newspapers that the Weaver appointment, while laudable, was only a compensation for the fact that Kennedy did not put a Negro in his Cabinet. In the second place, Weaver had once belonged to organizations listed as Communist fronts; this gave Southerners an excuse other than his race to oppose him. And in the third place, Weaver was on record as favoring an immediate executive order forbidding racial discrimination in any federal housing project; Kennedy's economic advisors opposed a prompt order because they were certain this would sharply curtail building and add to the recession which gripped the nation at the time.

Almost lost was the fact that Weaver was eminently qualified for the housing job. He had served in the Housing Authority during the New Deal days, he had been New York's state Rent Administrator, and he had been on New York City's Housing and Redevelopment Board. His membership in the Communist fronts was easily explained: During the depression days all civil rights organizations were either started by Communists or soon joined by them, and yet it was only natural that a Negro of Weaver's liberal leanings would belong to such groups. He had no Communist connections after that period.

His nomination was approved by the Senate, and he took charge of the federal housing programs.

Chapter Sixteen

THE CONGRESS

FOR ALL THE executive powers of the White House, the President is invariably hamstrung if he doesn't have the support of Congress. He must be able to get his appropriations granted, his appointments confirmed, and his new laws passed if he is going to fashion any kind of program.

Thus the relations between the White House and Capitol Hill always are important. The President must be equipped to exert influence when he faces a pressing need to get a bill through, and yet he must be cautious not to run afoul of Congressional jealousy over its prerogatives.

Most Presidents begin with a head start in their relationships with Congress. The new President usually brandishes a clear-cut mandate from the voters, which results in a "Congressional Honeymoon" during which Representatives and Senators dare not balk the will of the people.

Kennedy did not enjoy this luxury. The margin of his victory was so narrow that Congressmen who opposed his policies felt they had as much a mandate as he had. But he was able to make up for this in part by quickly creating the image of a strong President. The nation had not seen such strength since Franklin Roosevelt. Harry Truman was variously handicapped by Republican Congresses, his lame-duck status, and a host of other factors. Dwight Eisenhower also had an opposition Congress but, more important, he did not believe in a strong executive. To establish himself as a man of strength, Kennedy quickly hurled at the Congress a series of concrete legislative proposals and then began plumping hard for their passage.

Since the Democrats hold comfortable majorities in both the House and the Senate, it would appear that a Democratic President should have no troubles with Congress, but in Washington things aren't that simple.

Although the Senate is composed of 65 Democrats and 35 Republicans, the real split on most legislation comes not between Democrats and Republicans but between conservatives and liberals. The Republicans are most likely to stick together, and when they do, their 35 votes, combined with the votes of 22 Southerners, form a conservative coalition which holds a 57 to 43 margin against the liberals.

In the House the Democrats have an official 262 to 175 edge. The liberals claim they are in command, even when a conservative coalition forms, because they can muster their own combine for a total of 210 to 220 votes. Yet, even with 22 Republicans voting against their leadership, the liberals won the 1961 Rules Committee fight by only five votes and lost the minimum-wage bill, a Kennedy favorite.

Furthermore, the seniority system of Congress puts the conservative Southerners at the head of the most vital committees. In the Senate the Finance Committee, which considers such matters as tax bills, Social Security bills and tariffs, has as its chairman Harry Byrd of Virginia. The chairman of the Judiciary Committee, which gets civil rights legislation, is Senator James Eastland of Mississippi. The Agriculture Committee is headed by Senator Allen Ellender of Louisiana, and the Banking and Currency Committee chairman is Senator Robertson of Virginia. In the House the Rules Committee, which is the traffic cop for many important bills, has as its chairman Representative Howard Smith of

Virginia. The Ways and Means Committee, which originates tax legislation, has Representative Wilbur Mills of Arkansas as its chairman, and the Armed Services Committee, Representative Carl Vinson of Georgia.

With the Congress so stacked for the conservatives, how has Kennedy passed any of his liberal legislation? And how can he get another bill through as long as he remains in office?

The answer lies in the weakness of the labels. Just as the Democrats and Republicans are split into liberals and conservatives, so the liberals are split into "very liberal" and "moderate," and the conservatives are split into "modern conservative" and "reactionary." Then, too, any Congressman may be liberal on one subject and conservative on another. Eastern Congressmen, for example, invariably vote liberal on civil rights no matter what their party or how they vote on money legislation.

It is just as easy to get Republican Senators Clifford Case of New Jersey, Jacob Javits of New York, or John Sherman Cooper of Kentucky to cross the party line and vote with liberal Democrats as it is to get Senators Eastland and Byrd to join with the conservative Republicans.

Officially, the Kennedy forces in the Senate are headed by Majority Leader Mike Mansfield of Montana and Assistant Majority Leader (or "Whip") Humphrey of Minnesota, with Senator Claude Smathers of Florida assigned to command of the Southern wing. In practice, things work out somewhat differently.

Vice President Johnson is the true leader in the Senate. Although he repeatedly pledges himself to stick to the executive branch of the government and not interfere with Congress beyond his official duties as presiding officer of the Senate, he moves in to take command at any moment of crisis.

He has the skill, the reputation, and the personality which is required.

Mansfield does not have either the temperament or the inclination to operate as Johnson did and does. To get things done, the majority leader must often make a common peace between such extremes as Republican Minority Leader Everett Dirksen of Illinois and fiery liberal leader Humphrey. That takes a bit of doing.

Before Johnson was elected Vice President, Mansfield served as Assistant Leader and it became obvious then that he was no Lyndon Johnson. Once when Johnson took off for Texas the Senate assembled on a Saturday morning and had to adjourn 15 minutes later because it was so tied up in a wrangle over procedure. That was the sort of thing Johnson always straightened out; Mansfield couldn't handle it at all.

This does not mean that Mansfield is an incompetent or a bust in the Senate. Far from it. It means only that he is not the Lyndon Johnson type of leader.

Johnson likes to operate in secrecy. He doesn't believe in Democratic caucuses which might produce nosy questions about his strategy or, even worse, suggestions for directing legislation through the Senate's traffic maze. He prefers to keep his plans to himself until he is ready to spring them on a surprised and, he hopes, stunned Senate.

Mansfield is different. He is inclined to tell his plans to his colleagues and to listen to them in the event that they have different ideas.

Johnson believes in a spurt-and-coast Senate. Especially when difficult legislation is on the horizon, Johnson likes to hold the vote off until the last moment and then attempt to ramrod the bill through. Part of his highly touted genius for compromise rests simply in getting the Senate so desperate to do *something* that the members eagerly seize any reasonable compromise that will dispense with the issue.

Mansfield believes in an even flow of legislation. He is more the idealist than Johnson. He likes to think of the Senate as deliberating on a bill and then casting a reasoned vote, rather than making a flash decision on a piece of legislation which was jerry-built at midnight.

Ideologically, Mansfield is a splendid floor leader for Kennedy. He and the Senator share the same moderate approach on just about every issue of the day. Mansfield has another trait of the ideal floor leader: He believes it his duty to back the administration's bills no matter how he may feel personally. He takes seriously his designation as the President's deputy in the Senate.

He is, in other words, the ideal Majority Leader for routine matters—as long as Johnson is there to handle the emergencies. And as Majority Leader he heads off many party splits which would certainly occur had a Humphrey from the left or a Southerner from the right been selected for the job.

Under the present setup there is Johnson to direct behind the scenes, Mansfield to operate on the floor, Humphrey to marshal the liberal wing, and Smathers to do the same for the Southern wing. But beyond this official leadership there is the real power of the Senate, and it does not always rest in the hands of those who appear to be at the top. For all Smathers' designation as chief of the Southerners, for example, their real leader is Richard Russell of Georgia. Then, too, in any money legislation Senator Byrd will follow no leadership except his own.

On the other hand, Kennedy frequently can count upon Case, Javits, and Cooper in his efforts to get liberal legislation passed. As a matter of fact, when personal friends are differentiated from political friends, Cooper is one of Kennedy's closest pals in the Senate.

In the House venerable Speaker Sam Rayburn heads up the Democratic forces, with Representative John McCormack of Massachusetts as the Majority Leader and Representative Carl Albert of Oklahoma as the whip.

Rayburn, the bald and cherubic bachelor from Texas, is a Washington institution. He has served 25 terms in the House, ten of them as Speaker. "I love this House," he says. "It is my life." And it is, too. Without wife or children, he stops working only to sleep.

Above all, Rayburn believes in party regularity. Although a Texan and consequently at least part-Southerner, he nevertheless spits stinging epithets at those Dixie Democrats who buck the party because of their position on civil rights. He is especially unforgiving of those who failed to support Truman, Stevenson, or Kennedy in national elections. "Those Dixiecrats are as welcome around here as a bastard at a family reunion," Rayburn snapped after the revolt against Truman in 1948.

Rayburn has walked the party line straighter than ever since Joe Martin was deposed as Minority Leader by the Republicans in 1958. At least Rayburn had an old and close friendship with Martin, even though they were on opposite sides of the aisle politically. There is no such tie with Minority Leader Charles Halleck of Indiana. Rayburn will deal with Halleck when he feels he must in the interest of efficiency, but this is something which appears a bit distasteful to him.

With the compulsion to label each Congressman, Rayburn could not be classed as a liberal, although he is an old-fashioned New Dealer. He is best described as a "national Democrat," that is, a man who considers the Democrats to be the party of the people, with neither regional nor racial exceptions.

Rayburn's idea of the perfect leader was Franklin Roosevelt. On the day that Roosevelt died, William L. White of the *New York Times* came upon Rayburn weeping in his office in the Capitol. At that moment, White subsequently wrote, Rayburn "took an oath for the future. Its substance was that Sam Rayburn, Southern Democrat and all, had followed Franklin Roosevelt in life and would follow Franklin Roosevelt in death."

Even more than Mansfield in the Senate, Rayburn believes that the House leadership has no choice but to follow the leadership of the President, no matter who is in the White House. The President was put there in a national election, and his Congressional leadership has no right to question the mandate, Rayburn feels. He expressed this view quite succinctly when he was addressing a group of Southern Democrats threatening to revolt against Harry Truman. "He is our leader or we have none," Rayburn said.

It was with this attitude that Rayburn automatically took command as Kennedy's chief deputy in the House. There are basic issues on which Rayburn differs with Kennedy, particularly on the matter of the federal government contributing money toward teachers' salaries. But the responsibilities of leadership are those which Rayburn places first. Furthermore, he had no time to ponder the degree of his support for Kennedy, since he had to back the administration in a nasty fight in the very first weeks of Kennedy's first Congress: That was on the decision to water down the power of the Rules Committee chairman. Rayburn immediately accepted the White House decision to go through with this, even though the Rules Chairman, Howard Smith, had been engineered into that job in the first place by none other than Sam Rayburn.

Rayburn's power in the House is intensified by his talent

for persuasion. He is not so much the devious manipulator in the manner of his protégé Lyndon Johnson as he is the spellbinder and the charmer. One Congressman who had announced his intention of voting against Rayburn told of holding his own through a full morning's argument. "But then I went to lunch and he called me back into his office before I could finish my dessert. I finally gave in. You just can't hold out against Rayburn. He put it on the basis of party loyalty and patriotic duty. If I hadn't agreed I'd be feeling like a renegade and a traitor."

Representative McCormack, the Majority Leader on the House floor, is in a peculiar position because he has long been a close ally of Rayburn and a bitter enemy of Kennedy. Although they are both from Massachusetts, there has been a certain coolness between Kennedy and McCormack ever since Kennedy first entered the House as a freshman Congressman in 1946. Elder statesman McCormack, who was first elected to Congress in 1928, sought to take young Kennedy under his wing, but Kennedy would have none of it. He was going his own way.

When McCormack rounded up a petition of Massachusetts Congressmen, both Republican and Democratic, to get President Truman to pardon the jailed Boston Mayor James Curley, only Kennedy refused to sign it. The real split came in 1956. Kennedy was backing Stevenson for President. McCormack agreed to go along with Truman's choice, Averell Harriman. McCormack entered himself in the state's preferential primary and, without opposition, he was designated as a favorite-son candidate. But this is not binding, and Kennedy meanwhile had sewed up the entire delegation for Stevenson. McCormack, the "favorite son," was left holding nothing but a bag of anger.

But the old man got his revenge. After Stevenson was

nominated, Kennedy and Senator Estes Kefauver were locked in their tight ballot for the Vice Presidential nomination. The first ballot was ending and the swing suddenly appeared to be to Kennedy: Arkansas switched its vote to Kennedy, then Kentucky, then New Jersey, then South Carolina! A stampede was beginning. Desperately McCormack signaled his old pal, Rayburn, the presiding officer, to recognize Senator Tom Hennings of Missouri. Hennings rose and switched Missouri's vote to Kefauver. That stopped the stampede. The nomination went to Kefauver and Kennedy was out in the cold—for the time being.

The bitterness between the two remains, but in Congress McCormack will always follow Rayburn's lead, even if it is in the interests of John Kennedy. When McCormack first entered the House, he decided that the best way to get ahead was to ingratiate himself with the Southerners, who controlled the Congress even more then than they do now. He was advised to move into the Washington Hotel because John Nance Garner lived there. McCormack did, and has lived in the same hotel ever since. He cozied up to Garner, to John Bankhead, and to Rayburn when the Texan became Speaker upon Bankhead's death.

McCormack follows the Rayburn lead on almost all votes, but he performs invaluable services on his own. He is, for one thing, the Northern axis of a Rayburn-McCormack, North-South leadership. He is the soother, the settler of petty differences.

Columnist George Dixon wrote of having lunch with McCormack in the Capitol one day: "In less than eight minutes I watched him settle nine different problems. From the entrance to the House restaurant to his favorite alcove is 19 feet. It took us 31 minutes to travel it. In that short distance the Majority Leader shook two score hands and stopped at seven different tables for quick discussion and held eight standup conferences with key Democratic Congressmen."

In addition to the official leadership, Kennedy has his own contacts in the House. Two of them, Representative Dick Bolling of Missouri and Representative Frank Thompson of New Jersey, are especially close to the President personally and become key figures whenever important administration legislation is before the House.

Adam Clayton Powell, the erratic Congressman from Harlem, holds a key position as chairman of the House Labor Committee. It was necessary for Kennedy to woo him at the start of the 1961 Congress, for many important administration bills will pass through his hands.

The Republican-Southern coalition is a constant headache to Kennedy in the House. Representative Smith of Virginia automatically became an enemy when his control of the Rules Committee was diluted. Representatives Carl Vinson of Georgia and Clarence Cannon of Missouri, two arch-conservatives, rank among the true powers of the House, especially in money matters. These men ally themselves often with the Republican majority to oppose Kennedy legislation, and usually they can lead more than a few supporters across the party line.

Kennedy wields as much power as he dares when key legislation is before the Congress. Significantly, he placed the same man in charge of both patronage and Congressional liaison when he first set up his staff. That is one weapon. His Cabinet members also make their discreet telephone calls to members when a vote is pending. Secretary Udall's discretion in assigning Interior Department projects makes him a particularly potent force among Western Congressmen, for example.

But the relations between Congress and the White House are seldom pat, with one completely dominating the other. It is very much a matter of give-and-take on both sides, which is, after all, pretty much what the founding fathers intended.

Chapter Seventeen

THE NATIONAL CHAIRMAN

SHORTLY AFTER the election Senator Keating, a Republican from New York, got the news. He would have to leave the charming gate house he had been renting in the Georgetown section of Washington. The owner, Mrs. Thurmond Chatham, said she had promised to rent the house to her old friend John Bailey if the Democrats won.

Keating snorted, "Okay, but that probably is the only campaign promise which will be kept." And then he added, "At least the Democrats have the courage of their evictions."

That gate house was not the only place where John Bailey might live in Washington, but it was obvious he would have to set up somewhere in the capital city as soon as John Kennedy became President. For Bailey, the Connecticut state chairman of the Democratic Party, was a prime mover in the successful campaign and it was certain that Kennedy would require his presence near by for a number of years.

Bailey promptly was named Democratic National Chairman. As such he is an important ex-officio member of the government, for Kennedy has stated quite frankly that as President he intends to remain very much in politics and especially in Democratic Party politics. There is about Kennedy none of the "above the battle" pose which General Eisenhower struck when he was elected President.

The New Frontier is supposedly populated with a different breed—with a dynamic young intellectual politico who smokes

filter-tip cigarettes rather than the traditional stogies. John
Bailey doesn't fit in here. There's nothing different about his
breed. He is the old-fashioned type of political boss who
sticks to his cigars and his smoke-filled rooms and his one-
syllable words.

He's bald and he wears conservative suits with vests and
he thinks that precinct organization is the most important
factor in politics. The only way he differs from the traditional
political boss is that he can't remember names to save his soul.
One political reporter back in Hartford said, after a few
years' acquaintanceship with Bailey, "I think he's getting to
know me—he's blowing his cigar smoke my way now." Actually, Bailey is so bad about remembering names that he has
worked out a substitute. He remembers places. So when he
sees a familiar face and can't, as usual, recall the name he
says, "And how are things in Chicago?" That usually works.
If the man isn't from Chicago, Bailey at least has a fighting
chance that maybe the chap visited Chicago lately.

Bailey has two principal jobs in the Kennedy administration: to handle patronage and to gird the party for future
elections. Even when Kennedy was inaugurated the Democratic National Committee was muttering about patronage.
It was not so much that the members objected to the men
Kennedy had already hired for his government as that no one
seemed to know just how the jobs were awarded and who
was the "man to see." Kennedy promptly fixed that with
Bailey's election—selection, really, since he was hand picked
by the President.

All federal jobs, including the vacancies for federal judge
and U.S. District Attorney, go through Bailey now. The only
exceptions are the ambassadorships and the regulatory
agency positions.

But Bailey is more than a hiring boss. He has also as his

task the rebuilding the Democratic Party in Kennedy's image. His first step was to point out the party's change in mission. He said upon his election: "The functions of the party organization and its chairman vary as the party is in and out of office. For the past eight years yeoman service has been rendered in achieving the image of a progressive fighting opposition. Now with the achievement of the highest office in the land our chief job is to strengthen and rebuild our party within the framework of the New Frontier. We have each of us a job to do . . . to recruit enlightened, attractive and intelligent volunteers and to increase the effectiveness of party workers."

Or, to state it more simply, when the party is out of power it is on the offensive, attacking the ins; and when it gets into power it must rebuild as a defensive organization to stave off the hungry outs.

Bailey started with a vast reorganization of the party's national headquarters in Washington. He wanted a stronger organization. His predecessor, Paul Butler, had operated a one-man show and Bailey wanted exactly the opposite: a large staff operating at several levels and on different missions all at the same time.

Bailey had one specific aim, to make the party "respectable —a party people are not ashamed to belong to especially in the suburbs." He planned also to scotch once and for all the Lyndon Johnson idea: that the Democratic Party should primarily be the party of the South and the West rather than the party of the Eastern minorities. Kennedy and Bailey hold the other view: that the Democratic Party has those Eastern minorities as its hard core and that there should be no sacrifice of them for the South.

The political lines of power now are plain. From the top the power from Kennedy funnels down through Larry O'Brien at the White House to Bailey at Democratic Headquarters and thence to the state chairmen and city organizations. There are to be no in-betweens. Butler had organized the Democratic Advisory Council to give the Stevenson liberals a public voice between elections when otherwise only the voices of the Congressional conservatives might be heard. The Council never had any authority, for the Congressional leadership refused to recognize it, but at any rate Bailey scrapped it because he didn't want any rival voices competing with the President for attention.

Bailey stepped into the most thankless job in politics with his eyes wide open. The National Chairman is forever pilloried for shortcomings, whether they be failure to pass major legislation or failure to get a postmastership for somebody's third cousin. Kennedy was only half joking when he told the Committee, "I will feel that he is doing a good job when you all say, 'Well, Kennedy is all right but Bailey is the one who is really making the mistakes.' That's the way it was in Connecticut. Governor Ribicoff was never wrong. It was always Bailey's fault. So that's what he's going to do down here in Washington."

Bailey agrees with that assessment. His attitude is "the administration is always right" and should never be questioned. He also feels that the National Chairman should pretty much keep his mouth shut. Butler, on the other hand, was constantly getting in hot water for publicly declaiming his own political opinions, but the new Chairman won't get himself into the same situation. He says, "When Lodge was governor of Connecticut I did the heckling and the razzing. When Ribicoff was elected I kept quiet. He made all the policy and the speeches. That's the way it will be with Jack in the White House. . . . I just talk to the guys no one else has time to talk to."

Bailey does considerable handholding with the machine

bosses. "I come up from the precincts myself," he explains. "They know they can talk to me. I've had all their problems myself."

He is addressing himself particularly to the Democratic Party's weak spots. When he went into headquarters for the first time, there awaited him a stack of reports from the Kennedy campaign staff on the areas they thought needed special attention. These vary quite a bit. They run from New York, where the reform leaders are fighting Tammany Hall, to the Midwest, where the Democrats lost in 1960 most of the new Congressional seats they had won in 1958, to the mountain states, where Kennedy posted his most disappointing showing of the election.

Bailey came up as Connecticut political boss the hard way. He was born November 23, 1904, in Hartford, the son of a contractor, but his father died when John was 13. The boy had to go to work to support his family, but he made it through Catholic University and the Harvard Law School and then went into politics.

He has had a variety of jobs, including executive secretary for both mayors and governors, city court judge, and legislature committee clerk. But only once has he run for elective office and he was beaten then. In 1940 he ran for probate judge. Despite Franklin D. Roosevelt's sweep that year, Bailey was the only Democrat in Hartford to lose. The margin was 15,000 votes.

He decided then to be a behind-the-scenes man, and that's what he has been ever since. He was elected chairman of the state Democratic committee in 1946 but thrown off the next year. He decided to make a fight for control. In a bitter battle with Thomas J. Spellacy he won back his chairmanship in 1947 and has held the job ever since. He refused to relinquish it, even when he was elected National Chairman.

Bailey has a law firm, Bailey and Wechsler, which has netted him a fortune. His opponents say a good bit of this money comes from lobbyists who know where their law business ought to go if they want anything done in Connecticut. Bailey concedes that the firm is employed by lobbyists but insists his partners handle that end of it and that he does not share in the income.

At any rate, Bailey became *the* political boss in Connecticut. He helped engineer Chester Bowles into the governor's office (although Bowles has always remained as aloof as he dared from the boss tactics) and he was the man behind Abraham Ribicoff.

Bailey has always found a very simple solution to any political problem. For example, he and Ribicoff were all set to eliminate the county governments and thus streamline Connecticut's administrative operations considerably when an unexpected hitch developed. Although plans were made for the state to absorb all county employees, the elected sheriffs suddenly rose up in objection. They had been in charge of the jails. Now the state was taking over the jails. What would happen to them? They began lobbying powerfully against the reform.

Bailey swiftly came up with a typically Bailey solution. He ordered written into the bill a provision that the state would appoint a special deputy jailer in each county. He assured the sheriffs that each would get the appointment in his home county. The sheriffs withdrew their opposition, the bill passed, and everyone was happy, even if a bit of the streamlining was sacrificed.

Although there was no doubt that Bailey was a true boss, many in the state thought he was a good one. The Hartford *Courant* said in an editorial: "At one time or another he has backed more than one candidate, not because he liked the individual but merely because he felt that this individual had the best chance of winning. This is a kind of intellectual discipline not all political leaders have been able to acquire. Instead many of them make the mistake of picking candidates whose views, background and record are sympathetic with their own and not necessarily with the voters."

Bailey was on the Kennedy bandwagon early. He first met the young Senator in 1954 when Kennedy was invited to address the state Democratic convention, the same convention which nominated Ribicoff for governor the first time. Bailey was impressed by what he saw.

As the *Courant* said, Bailey is a man who ties himself to a winner. In 1948 Bailey had plumped hard to get General Eisenhower as the Democratic Presidential nominee, and now he saw in young Kennedy an opportunity to become a national kingmaker.

Bailey was one of the key men in Kennedy's bid for the Vice Presidential nomination in the 1956 National Convention. The so-called "Bailey Paper" was a treatise actually prepared by Kennedy's staff but distributed by Bailey to the delegates to argue that a Roman Catholic could get elected. With Ribicoff operating on the floor and Bailey in the wings, they came within 20½ votes of landing the nomination for Kennedy.

They left Chicago not in despair but convinced that the good showing should send them after the bigger prize, the Presidential nomination, in 1960. They started work almost immediately.

Today he recalls, "At the 1957 and 1958 national governors' conferences they laughed and asked Ribicoff if I were serious about talking Kennedy for President. At the 1959 conference they said Jack would be fine for Vice President. And at the

1960 conference, just before the Democratic convention, the same ones were asking whether Jack would make it on the first or on the second ballot."

Bailey traveled the nation working for Kennedy, first for the nomination and then for the Presidency. He spent a full month in West Virginia before that state's decisive preferential primary. He directed the political operation for Kennedy's bid in the New Hampshire primary, and he led the safari which induced Governor Mike DiSalle to pledge Ohio's vital convention votes to Kennedy.

After Kennedy was nominated it was obvious to the professional politicians just who should replace Butler as the National Chairman for the forthcoming campaign. The bosses especially—Jake Arvey of Illinois, David Lawrence of Pennsylvania, and Carmine DeSapio of New York—called for Bailey's immediate election.

But the Kennedy camp vetoed it. This was not a case of ingratitude. It was a case of being prudent. Like Kennedy, Bailey is a Roman Catholic, and with the religious issue so obvious a thorn it was decided to let Bailey operate without any official title. Senator Henry Jackson of Washington agreed to head up the national committee only for the duration of the election campaign. Then, it was agreed, he would resign and permit Bailey to take over, especially if Kennedy were elected.

As he did during the primaries, Bailey toured the nation working for Kennedy for President. He was the mender of fences. Where Bobby Kennedy moved in with his demands and his pep talks and his calls for more and faster action, Bailey followed through with the organizational work. He could, after all, talk to the state chairmen about their precinct problems.

As the party's National Chairman, he is continuing that work. He commutes about once a week back to Connecticut, where he retains both his law firm and his political authority. But mostly John Bailey operates in the big time now. The State-House political boss has made it to the White House.

Chapter Eighteen

THE KENNEDY GOVERNMENT

JUST AS EACH MAN has his background, his beliefs, and his personality, so the Kennedy government as a whole has its background, beliefs, and personality.

It is a young administration, the youngest in our country since McKinley was President. The average age of the Cabinet is 47, but even going beyond this statistic the administration has a youthful look: its policy makers are, on the whole, lean and active men, skiers and tennis players as well as touch football players, with seldom even the first touches of gray.

It is a wealthy administration. Some, like the Kennedys, were born to great sums of money. Others, like Secretary of Commerce Hodges, rose from the meanest poverty to amass their own fortunes. But, on the whole, the top-level men came to Washington no longer concerned about the weekly paycheck.

It is an intellectual administration. The jokes are all about Harvard, and indeed one-third of the first-rank appointments went to Harvard men. But, more important, is the intellectual attitude of the administration. This calls for study, for the continual search for new ideas and new approaches to the old problems. It calls for dependence upon university economists rather than Chamber of Commerce boosters in any analysis of business conditions, present and future. It calls for taking long-range views of immediate problems.

It is an administration of minorities. There are two Jews, a Catholic, and a Mormon on the Cabinet alone. The President, of course, set the tone for this when he became the first Catholic to inhabit the White House, but there appears to be even more significance than that: There appears in Washington now an atmosphere of emancipation, an attitude that the man is more important than his background.

It is a moderate administration. The idea appears to be to achieve liberal aims by conservative means. The left-wingers are all right-wing and the right-wingers are all left-wing: the Secretary of Labor was a union attorney who often had to show his clients the management's side in order to break stalemates; the Secretary of Commerce was a big-business governor whose greatest exploit was the development of small business in his state. The President himself is a man of caution. Not only does he look before he leaps, but often he sends an emissary down first to determine how cold the water is.

It is an administration with political savvy. Even the amateurs are professionals in that they have been students or professors of government if not active participants. The experience of the administration's policy makers in government is far out of ratio to their ages. Many in their 40's have been in government or politics for 20 years. The administration thinks that over the years this political savvy will circumvent many bitter showdowns; it thinks it has the skill and experience to soften up both the electorate and the Congress before any old policies are reversed or before any unpleasant legislation is submitted.

It is an eager-beaver administration. It is composed of men who consider the working day 10, 12, or 14 hours long. It is composed of men who are driving bosses and demanding masters. It is composed of men who are genial when things go right, but who are tough and hard when things go wrong.

These are the Kennedy men. But while we may speak of "the Kennedy administration" or "the Kennedy government," it must be remembered that the crew brought in by the new President, any new President, is only a small part of the United States government. It is true that Kennedy had 6,000 jobs to fill. But it is also true that 2,500,000 men and women work for the government.

These people must execute the orders of the policy makers or else the orders become a sham. It is all very well for Postmaster General Day to promise a cheerful and efficient postal system, but if the mailman on the route growls and stops to rest every ten minutes, the policy has been circumvented.

One big objective of the administration is to assure the compliance of orders. This isn't easy. It means following up not once but frequently to determine that the new policies remain in effect. It means assigning competent men to observe each department at the working level and yet not wreck morale with a gumshoe psychology.

Professor Neustadt, in his book *Presidential Power: The Politics of Leadership,* cited the power of persuasion, the concern for professional reputation in Washington, and the desire for public prestige as the three forces which make a strong President. This goes beyond the White House. It extends into every policy-making department of the government. Secretary of Labor Goldberg must persuade union and management opposites to accept government compromises; he cannot force them to do so. Secretary of the Treasury Dillon must maintain a professional reputation in the financial community, lest all his policies be deprecated and in effect defeated. Secretary of Defense McNamara must maintain public prestige or else he cannot make the necessary demands on the nation's manpower and pocketbook.

The Kennedy administration is acutely aware of these needs. It will, for this reason, concentrate on the art of persuasion and also on the art of public relations. The so-called Madison Avenue tactics of the Eisenhower administration were often decried by these same men who are now in office. They were sincere. They are now using the same techniques for their own ends.

Whereas the Eisenhower administration public relations effort was largely directed to minimizing each problem and assuring the nation that everything was just great, the Kennedy approach is to tell everyone that things are in a hell of a mess but can be straightened out. A great part of this effort lies in the art of persuasion: if the people are convinced things are in a mess, they are more likely to accept the legislation deemed necessary to set things right. Part of it builds professional reputation: it creates an atmosphere of knowing, competent men at the helm, ready to steer the ship through the storm. Part of it maintains public prestige: it heads off the deflated feeling which might otherwise come if the public were to awaken one morning to find that the administration which supposedly had everything in hand was suddenly caught short by a nasty problem.

The national politics of the Kennedy administration constitutes a balance of the old and the new. It is built, of course, on the Democratic Party, that incongruous mixture of the Negro wards up North and the segregation-forever precincts down South. One reason for the Kennedy moderation is the preservation of this uncomfortable but effective and historic coalition.

Throughout the four or eight years of Kennedy in the

White House, there will be a cautious intermingling of the old pros of the Democratic organization with the young Kennedy men. The object will be to avoid alienating the old pros and yet to temper them with an infusion of young eager beavers with horn-rimmed glasses—the Kennedy type. The organizations which Kennedy built within the Democratic Party to further his fight for the nomination are not being scrapped; these people have been carefully cultivated into permanent outposts, fed by patronage and deference so that they will stand ready to serve again. They are not encouraged to declare war on the hoary Democratic machines of their localities, when such machines exist, but they are indeed given discreet encouragement when they launch battle on their own. The administration was not yet in power when it made known its support of Democratic insurgents against Manhattan's Tammany Hall, even though Kennedy actually owed more political loyalty to Tammany—before the convention these insurgents were supporters of Adlai Stevenson while Tammany was solidly behind John F. Kennedy.

Another facet of the Kennedy administration is its disdain for red tape. Here again is the impetuosity of youth. The President himself has set the tone of the administration by popping uninvited into meetings and conferences.

There is a point to all of this. It is not disrespect for tradition, but it is a disdain for the past, especially the more recent past. Kennedy frequently calls for "new ideas." As a matter of fact, the very word "idea" has become a credo of the administration.

Kennedy has learned that often there appear to be no new ideas. He assigned a series of teams to present special reports and recommendations before his inauguration. The work was done by experts, often academic experts, outside the government. Yet the President-elect was disappointed that few really new suggestions came from these reports. Too often the reports simply restated the known problem and then pleaded for a solution. There was no doubt, for example, that James Landis analyzed the problem of the regulatory agencies with absolute accuracy, but his report offered no concrete method of reform. He did call for a higher quality of commissioner, but he did not reveal what these men should do or where they would be found or how they would be induced to join the government.

Nevertheless, the crusade for ideas can hardly be written off as a failure. The crusade has encouraged men within the administration to speak up and not fear the label of nonconformist.

The fact remains, however, that the successes the administration enjoyed in its first months were successes of action rather than of ideas. The Defense Department stepped up its quick-striking force almost immediately. The Labor Department stepped up its aid to the unemployed almost immediately. These were not new approaches but simply old approaches which had been forsaken by the previous administration.

They did signify the stress on efficiency, however—on getting things done the fastest and most practical way. That is a primary Kennedy objective. He seeks to eliminate the endless round of conferences and committee meetings which have plagued Washington more with each succeeding administration. He feels that more can be done with one crisp order than in two days of round-table discussion. One White House aide said the most difficult thing about Cabinet meetings was "thinking up something for them all to discuss." On the surface, a Cabinet meeting sounds very important. But just what problems does the Secretary of Agri-

culture have to discuss with the Postmaster General? Even
if one should arise, why must the Secretary of Defense sit
there and endure it?

A Washington correspondent who returned from an extended European tour at inauguration time was asked just
what Europeans expected of the Kennedy administration.
"Too much," he replied.

That answer might hold for Americans, too. The arch Republicans of the nation expected too much in the way of
oppressive and confiscatory legislation from these wild super
liberals. The arch Democrats expected too much in the way
of old new deal panaceas from these saviors of the Republic.
The problems, domestic and international, are far too broad
and deep to be settled by any single administration, if indeed they are settled, to use the words of Kennedy's inauguration address, "in our days on this planet."

When Kennedy first won the nomination at the Democratic National Convention he envisioned a "first 100 days"
of the magnitude of the Franklin Roosevelt administration.
He said as much in his acceptance speech. But after the
election was won and time grew nigh for the inauguration
ceremony, the "first 100 days" idea was scrapped completely.

There was nothing that could be done in any 100 days.
Partly because of the make-up of the Congress and partly
through Kennedy's own inclinations of caution, there was
no series of sweeping bills which could be introduced. The
problems were not of that nature. The cold war can't be
ended by passing a new law. The missile gap can't be closed
by rushing through a new appropriation. Roosevelt could
close and reorganize the banks. Kennedy could not close
and reorganize the Congo.

The administration did show a burst of speed in the one
area where there was something in common with 1933. He

was ready with swift anti-recession measures. But this was a pale 100 days compared to FDR's baptism of fire.

The caution which marks the Kennedy administration has led some to feel that, in reality, this is no real change from the Eisenhower administration, that the color of the package is the only discernible difference. This is not true. The Kennedy administration does indeed have its own attitudes and its own policies which are unique.

Toward business, for example, there is not the hostility normally attributed to extreme liberals and there is not the chumminess which the Eisenhower administration maintained with the biggest of big business. Actually the Kennedy administration, largely because of the thinking of those professors, concerns itself more with *business conditions* than with businesses as entities. It has the theory that the government's function is the maintenance of full employment and wage standards; the businesses can take care of themselves if this healthy climate prevails. It wants to make business investments lucrative but not privileged: that was the idea behind seeking better tax write-offs for plant investment at the same time that the administration sought to plug tax loopholes which existed only for the benefit of certain industries.

The Kennedy administration is definitely liberal on welfare benefits, all the way from old-age medical insurance to federal aid for education. It is likewise liberal on the issue of civil rights, but here it is at the same time practical; it will at all times seek to circumvent any showdown with the Southern wing of Congress. In many ways this attitude could make for even more reforms over the years. Many Southern Congressmen who concede the inevitability, if not the justice, of integration must fight it on the floor of the House or Senate lest opponents back home massacre them in the next election. These same Congressmen are spared the ordeal if the same civil rights action is accomplished by executive order; they can damn the White House in one torrid speech and then resume normal business with clear conscience and a clear road to re-election. Thus the Kennedy administration wants to do as much as it possibly can on civil rights a mile or two away from Capitol Hill.

On defense, the Kennedy administration policy is to spend more than the Eisenhower administration. Under Eisenhower the balanced budget was supreme. Under Kennedy there is lip service to the balanced budget, but there is not nearly the sacrifice in defense research and procurement.

In the field of foreign policy the Kennedy administration is less unbending than the Eisenhower administration. President Eisenhower himself was deeply committed, inwardly as well as outwardly, to the cause of peace, and he was willing to go anywhere to further it. But the policies of John Foster Dulles allowed little room for maneuver. The millennium was a stalemate. The Kennedy foreign policy is to attempt give and take. This is a dangerous game, of course. Kennedy feels he must beware of giving and then finding nothing offered for him to take. But the strategy is being explored hopefully, if timorously.

During the four or, more likely, eight years that John Kennedy is President, those black heads of the Kennedy men will become tinged with gray and those touch football games will give way to more sedentary hobbies. Many burning hopes will become wistful memories. Kennedy himself is convinced that the years of his administration will decide the fate of the free world. He concedes that the fate may not be a happy one.

But if eagerness and conscientiousness and good intentions and long hours can be decisive, the future is good. For these are the qualities which the Kennedy administration is giving the world.

INDEX